LEGACY OF
Faith

LEGACY OF
Faith

BECKY CROASMUN

iUniverse, Inc.
Bloomington

LEGACY OF FAITH

The views expressed in this work are solely those of the author and do not necessarily reflect the views of the publisher, and the publisher hereby disclaims any responsibility for them.

iUniverse books may be ordered through booksellers or by contacting:

iUniverse
1663 Liberty Drive
Bloomington, IN 47403
www.iuniverse.com
1-800-Authors (1-800-288-4677)

Because of the dynamic nature of the Internet, any web addresses or links contained in this book may have changed since publication and may no longer be valid.

Any people depicted in stock imagery provided by Thinkstock are models, and such images are being used for illustrative purposes only.
Certain stock imagery © Thinkstock.

ISBN: 978-1-4620-3587-8 (pbk)
ISBN: 978-1-4620-3588-5 (ebk)

Printed in the United States of America

iUniverse rev. date: 07/09/2011

● *DEDICATED* ●

To Max, Emily, and David Bernheim for giving their lives to spread the Gospel of Jesus Christ.

To P. Hanson Jones for his love in also sharing the gospel, as well as helping to document the life story of Max.

To Mark, Esther, Ruth, John and Lois who through the years have shown everyone they met the same love for souls their parents did.

Faith: the constant assurance that what we hope for is going to happen. It is the evidence of things we cannot yet see.

神愛世人　　甚至將他的獨生子賜給他們

叫一切信他的　不至滅亡 反得永生 約翰福音3:16

For God so loved the world that he gave his only begotten Son, that whosoever believeth in him should not perish, but have everlasting life (John 3:16).

FORWARD BY
● BRIDGETT CROASMUN ●

I have heard the story of my great grandparents told and retold throughout my life until I knew the details by heart. I remember as a young child being completely enthralled by all things Chinese. My grandmother taught me how to eat with chopsticks the proper way, my great aunts Ruthie and Lollie (Lois) used to sing songs to me in Chinese. It was not uncommon to hear the words "When Grandpa was in China." spoken in our home. I also remember other words being spoken in our home, other stories, of total and complete dependence on God for our needs. Faith isn't an easy concept to master, but if any child was raised to know who their provider was, it was me. Faith is the absence of fear and the complete and utter trust in an unseen, but very well known God.

And as you read these letters, you may wonder how the entire family could generation after generation continue in the ministry started by my great grandparents? How after knowing the story of what they sacrificed, could we continue to serve a God who allowed these children to become orphans, who allowed the lives of these people to be snuffed out so early? But how could we allow their sacrifice to be in vain?

There have been many times in my life that I have faced insurmountable odds, with no hope, only to have my faith to see me thru. When others have failed me, I knew who to go to, because I had been taught from an early age to depend on my heavenly father for my every need. It was because of this legacy of faith that I never even considered any other option but to lean on the everlasting arms of Daddy God.

To experience life is to know pain. To experience love is to know heartbreak. To experience peace one must go thru turmoil. To experience solitude one must know loneliness. To experience joy, one must know sorrow. To really live life one must meet death. Not death of one's own self, but the darkness, fear and finality that brings death, the loss of love, the feeling of a shattered heart, the fear of never being loved. When one has known these things, then one can reach up for the only hand that truly holds us and be lifted from the depths of bitterness and despair and feel the comfort of healing.

In spring of 2010, as I began the semester at Life Pacific College, my Multi Cultural Evangelism Class assigned us the "Unreached Peoples Project". The goal was to work in conjunction with the Joshua Project Website and find a group of people anywhere in the world listed on the site as an unreached people group. I figured I had this in the bag; I was the great grandchild of missionaries. As I began my research, I found out something spectacular. The rural, area of the Chinese mountains that is now part of Burma, where my grandparents worked, lived and ministered, was primarily Christian. These people were no longer unreached. As I researched more and more, I found that for miles and miles in this rural area, in a country that is primarily Buddhist, the current primary religion was Christianity. I believe with my whole heart this is due, to the willingness of Max and Emily to go to a place and to a people that other missionaries would not travel.

Now as I prepare my sixteen-year old daughter to head off to Bible College to train become a missionary, I am reminded of those words spoken by Esther, "It could not have happened if God had not willed it".

It did not matter the opposition, the lack of finances, the lack of support, Max and Emily stepped out in faith, depending only on God. Our family has come full circle. "And this gospel of the kingdom will be preached in the whole world as a testimony to the nations, and then the end will come" Matthew 24:14.

• LEGACY OF FAITH •

This book consists of letters written by Alfred Max and Emily Bernheim. It is compilation of letters written by them describing ministry in China until their death in 1940. The source of these letters are from the Philadelphia Message a monthly newsletter produced by the Philadelphia Church which supported the Bernheim's while they were in China.

My grandparents gave their lives to be obedient to the will of God. I was privileged to get these letters and undertake the task of compiling them in a book. This is the legacy that my grandparents left me and all the family members who have lived since. I find myself asking "What will I do to continue this legacy and have I done my part in passing it on?"

Credit must also be given to Phillip Hanson Jones who was also a missionary in China and endured many hardships to spread the gospel. He helped my grandparents build the mission house they were living in when they died and also documented Alfred and Emily Bernheim's testimony so we would know about their early life.

So sit back and enjoy the story of the life of Alfred Max Bernheim (Max) and his conversion, his marriage to Emily and their call to carry the Good News of Jesus Christ to those who might never have heard it had my grandparents not been willing to sacrifice all they had.

Here is my Legacy of Faith. My prayer is that you will be blessed and grow in faith while reading this book.

• CHAPTER 1 •

My legacy did not begin with a family who had always been Christians. My grandfather began this legacy. His name was Alfred Max Bernheim (he went by Max). You have to know his story to fully understand my legacy. Here is his story as told by my grandfather to Philip Hansen Jones, a very close friend.

My parents were German. They emigrated to American when young. My father was very successful in business and made a lot of money. He became popular with the wrong kind of people. My mother loved social life and followed my father in all his dissipations. They drank and smoked and gambled and threw many wild parties, persisting in their folly and going from bad to worse until they were rarely sober.

My brother and I were the only children, I being seven and he just four years of age when they decided to dispose of us and be free to follow their wild life. They consigned us to the uncertain mercies of a convent and forgot us. No doubt I was very naughty, yet I hardly deserved the harsh punishments I received in that convent. I never saw my brother anymore and don't know what became of him. Sometimes I was locked in a dark room, without food, for three days. Sometimes they beat me cruelly. I hated them all and vowed to run away at the very first opportunity. That opportunity came about five years later.

They set me to work in the garden. The walls were very high and kept in good repair. The iron gates were big and very difficult to climb. How I loathed this place and everyone in it, yet there

1

seemed no hope of escape! I scanned every inch of those walls, seeking some climbable portion, in the very faint hope that I might find some way out of the barred and bolted building during the night. But the walls offered no hope of escape. Nevertheless I firmly believed that one day my chance would come, and it did.

I was working by the tall, iron front gate. The bell rang. A sister who carried a large bunch of keys around her waist opened the gate to let in a man driving a truck full of supplies. During the bustle and excitement and cross talk, with a pounding heart I slipped behind the truck then bolded into freedom. How I ran! I seemed to have run several miles before forced to stop to regain my breath. When sufficiently recovered, being in terror of pursuit, I ran and ran, on and on, not knowing where I was headed for. Thus I ran or walked and begged my way until I arrived in the city of Chicago.

In Chicago I became a pitiful little homeless waif, just a street urchin, begging or stealing every day in order to survive. I was smart and it did not take me long to learn the tricks of the trade. I excelled as a pickpocket. This was but the mere beginnings of a life of crime. Before I was fourteen I was smart enough to join up with a bunch of gangsters. Thus began my life of total crime. Before I was twenty-one, I had just about committed every crime on the calendar except murder, and it was only the mercies of God kept me from that. I toted a good gun and well knew how to use it, ready to do so any time. I was desperate and bitter and not afraid of anything; had already been involved in many hold ups and bank robberies. This gave me all the money I needed for reckless living, and I really went the pace in wickedness.

But at last the police began to catch up with me and I was spending far too much time behind the bars. Each sentence was longer and the last one was for five years. I became very discouraged with life and felt it would be better to be dead than spending so much time in the penitentiary. So during that last term I came to a decision. I decided that, when my time was up I would not return to crime but find a job and go straight. No one helped me to this decision; it was purely common sense asserting itself.

I moved from one job to another for various reasons. Once I was a motorman for a while on a city train, and was involved in a serious accident. Others got injured or killed but I escaped unscathed. Another time I was involved in a motor smash and this time also, some were seriously injured or killed but I was unhurt. Things of this kind have happened to a number of times and I was amazed for I seemed to lead a charmed life. Since I have come to know the Lord I can clearly now see that it was the devil trying to get me, but God did not permit it. He had a plan for my life and a purpose to fulfill.

Finally I took a job driving long distance trucks. One long day, the sun had been so hot, and toward evening I became very weary. As night came on I was ascending a steep incline and suddenly became very sleepy. I was still some miles from my intended destination so decided to finish the incline then find some convenient place to park on the roadside and take a short nap. But I fell dead asleep over the wheel. The truck ran over the edge and began to somersault downhill, flinging me out and rolling over me. No reason on earth why I wasn't crushed to death, just that God did not permit it. The devil took everything from Job except his life, and so it was with me.

Becky Croasmun

I awakened many hours later, in a hospital. What they told me seemed unbelievable. I had been picked up by the ambulance, lying on the grass with my stomach ripped open and my intestines lying on the grass by my side. I came very near to death that time, yet after several months of cruel suffering, patched up and penniless, they let me go. But go where? I had no friends, no home, no loved ones, no health, no money, no strength and no hope. I had nothing in this entire world but a broken body and a pair of wooden crutches. Filled with despair I hobbled on not knowing which way to turn.

It so happened that my mother's home was in this town and actually not far away from where I was. It afforded the only gleam of hope. I well know what a condition she had come through dissipation. However, after all, she was my mother and I was her son. I decided to visit her. Surely when she saw my pitiful condition she would be sorry for me, especially when she knows I have reformed and going straight now. Surely she would take me in. Thus, hopefully I hobbled up the approach to her home. The kitchen door was open so I dragged my ruined body through the door. My mother happened to be right there in the kitchen, and although it was only late noon she was already drunk. I tried to tell her my story, but as soon as she realized who I was she grabbed a sharp hatchet and with a string of oaths, flung it at me with all her force. It barely missed my ear and hitting the door with the blade it hung there, quivering, such had the power of her drunken madness. In fury she screamed, "Get out of here before I kill you!"

With dreadful despair in my heart I swung through the door on my crutches and hobbled back down the hill. What could I do?

Where could I go? To whom could I turn for sympathy and help? There was nowhere and nobody that I knew of in this whole wide world. No money, no friends, no health and no hope. I racked my brain for a solution but finally decided there was nothing left for me to do other than to commit suicide so with this solution of despair, I hoppled through the city toward the river.

Arriving at a crossing, I waited with others to cross the road. While waiting there, something very wonderful happened. It was Sunday evening, near to church going time, though in all the years, ever since I fled that convent, I had never been inside the doors of any church. However, unconsciously, the religious life of the convent had left an impression upon me. Suddenly, from somewhere over the rooftops came the beautiful sound of church bells. What a heavenly sound! It thrilled me until I hardly knew what I was doing. All stirred up and agitated I turned to the people around me and cried, "Church bells! The church! Tell me! Where it is? I want to go to church! I *must* go to church before I die!"

Right behind me stood a friendly and happy looking couple. It was they who answered me. "You wish to go to church brother? Praise the Lord; you may go with us for we are on the way. However, before going to church we mean to visit a poor brother who is dying of T.B. He lives right near here. If you care to come along with us we'll be glad to have you." That statement a poor brother dying of T.B. stirred me strangely. Someone else suffering and dying. Yes, I would be glad to go, and I compelled strength to walk faster. Then after seeing this other sufferer I would attend church before taking my life.

Together we crossed the road. They suited their stride to my cumbersome gait. I learned that they were Full Gospel Christians, but had no idea what that meant. However, I clearly sensed that they were kind, good people, and they impressed me with the feeling that they seemed to know God intimately. I had never met people like this before.

It was not far, and in a few minutes we arrived at the home of the sick young man. Ushered to his bed side, my heart was greatly stirred by the sight of his pitiful face of suffering. Only twenty one years of age and dying like this! My friends said, "Brother, shall we kneel down and ask God to help this friend? He needs God in a big way." A flood of compassion flowed through me from head to foot. I flung myself on my knees at the bedside and wailed in anguish of heart in behalf of this pitiful young man. Oh God! Have mercy on this poor young man! That was how I prayed, and remember, I knew nothing about real prayer. Who had I met in all of my life to teach me? I was very familiar with convent chanting and counting of beads and despised it. However, even that religion had created within my heart a belief in God though it had never been exercised. I had never heard the gospel and knew nothing about repentance. But I proved God to be far bigger than all formality.

"Oh God", I cried in desperate earnestness and wholehearted sincerity, "have mercy on this poor brother!" Many wouldn't believe it, but it is true! The Lord Jesus touched him and made him every whit whole right then and there. The Lord knew all about my sinful and unregenerate heart. He also knew that it was broken and bleeding by reason of what I had gone through and that such a heart was capable of being really touched with the very feelings of this poor man's infirmities. The Pharisees formed long and eloquent prayers but knew nothing about compassion. God never listened to them but he listened to the broken hearted appeal of this old sinner and healed that sufferer at once! It seems that compassion, as God sees it, is priceless, and how can we obtain it apart from a broken heart? So we all went to church and I tell you, it was a wonderful meeting. I got saved that night so forgot my appointment with the river. Praise the Lord!

Three weeks later, my two friends and I were kneeling down in their home for a few words of prayer before going to church. We prayed for the usual things, the presence of God, cleansing for the hearts of the saints, His blessed presence and the salvation of souls. Suddenly, once again those bells began to chime and they had the very same electrifying effect upon my spirit. These saints had been wonderful to me. They had received me into their home, fed and clothed me, treated me as if I were Jesus Himself. In return I sometimes drove their car for them as far as I was able. It had been three weeks of heaven on earth for me, a literal resurrection! I was happy all day long, always singing and praising the Lord. Wonderful days, but I never dreamed of the glory that was waiting for me, just around the corner!

Mightily moved by the sound of those chiming bells I leaped to my feet, and ran from the house. My friends rushed after me. I was already about one hundred yards away. "What is the matter? Where are you going", they cried? Agitated and greatly excited I stopped for one moment and answered, "To church of course, I cannot wait, *I must* go *now*!" But what about your crutches they cried? I lifted my hands and looked down at my sides in amazement. I had actually run all that way unaided. A great faith sprung up in my heart. I shouted back, "If I can run this far without them I can continue for the rest of the way." And so it was. In this amazing way I was healed and never used those pieces of wood again. Then God baptized me in the Holy Ghost and life became so sweet I felt no need of heaven.

• CHAPTER 2 •

After Max began to walk with the Lord, he met my grandmother Emily Hasenkraug according to Philip Hansen Jones in his book, I Beseech Thee.

Max was always exceptionally fervent. Having been forgiven much and having received much, he was always ready to leap to his feet to tell what the Lord had done for him. The testimony of such a brand plucked from the burning possessed inspiring vitality. One young lady was particularly impressed. Close friends told me that Emily was *born* good. Emily was a true and steadfast Christian well versed in the Word of God. She began to take a kindly interest in this rugged old one time criminal, now a saint and on fire for God, yet knowing very little about the Bible. Friends suggested that he sit at Emily's feet awhile for Bible study, and doing this, it was not long before he offered her his heart.

But Emily had refused similar offers from others and, although she was now very fond of him, would only accept his offer of marriage on one condition. These are Emily's words on that condition.

"Some years ago I felt God's call in my heart to go to China as a missionary. I don't know why, but it never came to pass, though the call has never left me. However, more recently I have felt a strong urge to be a missionary to the American Indians. I want to go and work among them on faith. If God will let us go together then we can be married. But not otherwise."

They prayed and asked the Lord to show His will and prove it by giving them a gospel caravan. This the Lord did, giving them other necessary things too. Thus they were married on a sunny, happy day on May 2, 1925 and they set out together to serve God among the Indians.

Several years later, with two small children, Mark and Esther, and the caravan just shaken into ruin over so many rough trails, they felt the need of asking the Lord to give them a larger one. The Lord met their need for this one also. Some years later, with three more children, Ruth, David, and John, they felt the time had come to ask the Lord for yet another caravan, still bigger than the last. But this time the Lord indicated to them that their work among the Indians was over and that now He meant to send them to China.

Max was most unwilling for this. He hadn't faith for such a long journey and didn't like the Chinese anyway. It depressed him so badly that he fell sick. In delirium he imagined he was in China and the bandits were cutting them all to pieces with big knives. But he recovered and finally became peacefully resigned to the revealed will of God. All their needs were supplied and they booked passage for seven on an ocean liner soon leaving for the Far East. It was truly a big venture of faith, but since God had planned it there was no risk incurred. God is infinitely more capable of meeting our needs than any board or committee.

A little while before leaving America, they took a farewell meeting in a simple little church run by a very devout group in Spokane, Washington. Emily got up to speak and this is what she said. "Dear friends, I have had the call of God for China, in my heart for many years, even long before I went to the American Indians. Now God has brought it to pass and I am very happy. I have laid everything, even my husband and children upon the altar. Last night I had a terrible dream! I dreamt I was in China holding my youngest baby in my arms when the bandits came and killed us. Even so, I take nothing back that I have given to God and am just as prepared to go whatever the cost."

After Emily had finished speaking it came Max's turn to speak. Standing to his feet, he related the facts of his illness and previous great fears and his present victory and complete readiness to do the will of God whatever the cost might be. Then he told them. "Like Emily, I too, last night, had a bad dream that does not leave me. I dreamed we were all in China and the bandits had slain my family. I was digging a grave for them with my bare hands. However, like Emily, I also feel peace and victory over this thing and have placed everything in God's hands." Thus, the whole family of seven left for China.

• CHAPTER 3 •

On-board the *Hikawa Mura*

To do dear ones in America:

Greetings in Jesus' precious name. We praise God from whom all blessings flow and they are flowing along with the great wide Pacific. Glory be to Jesus! We boarded ship August 10, 1936 with friends accompanying us to the ship. After taking the baggage and the children to our stateroom, we went on deck again to wait the starting of the ship. Clang! Clang! Clang! The sailor's hammer on a brown tin of some sort, the loads are on, the ship is ready, and the visitors must leave, at last all are off.

The gang plank is removed, and paper streamers are being thrown from the passengers to the folks left on the dock. Back and forth the roles of paper go amid shouting and laughter and tears. Slowly the ship begins to move, the crowds holding this streamers walk along with the boat to the end of the dock. At last all the paper ropes are broken and we with the ship turnaround. Goodbye America and loved ones. God is calling us to cross the Pacific. There are souls for whom Christ died on the other side that have not yet heard of the Savior's love. It is to these we go, that they may have the joy of sins forgiven.

We go forth in the Master's name; you are the rope holders. Much of what is to be done will mean be faithful! Look not to the right or to the left but keep your eyes on Jesus, the author and finisher of our faith.

The beds are *bunks* made of fancy wood, with board bottoms. Although there are no springs there is a mattress and a hard straw pillow. But we are tired and soon fall asleep, thankful to the Lord who had no place to lay his head. (The Bernheim's are traveling third class).

Our room is located so we do not hear the noise of the engine. The meals are good, the food abundant. Just a word to anyone who may follow us, we are well satisfied with the service, of course, if people want springs in their bed and a soft pillow, they had better take tourist cabin instead of third class. We furnish our own towels and wash basin and drinking cups for use in the state room.

I am typing in the dining room. A number of the crew marvel at my typewriter, it is so small that I can carry it in my hand yet with carbon paper I can write four letters at a time. They are Japanese and want to know all about it. I tell them it is a present from my friends in America. "Very good, very good", they say. If we speak slowly, they can understand us quite well.

The children have made friends with several Japanese children and have sung their gospel songs for a number of people on board. Who knows the end of all the songs that are sung to the honor and glory of God? Everyone listens while the children ask their blessings at the table and sing their praise songs.

Esther spent her ninth birthday on the boat. The chief baker baked a cake and there were many surprises that made today a happy one.

Becky Croasmun

The children were very anxious to see a whale and God granted their desire. It was wonderful. They went in bands and seem to follow a certain path, first one band than another and they all kept a certain distance between the whales.

Much of the voyage was stormy. We were somewhat seasick but, praise the Lord; He made it possible for us all to enjoy every meal.

At Yokohama, Japan

Yokohama is about 4307 miles from Vancouver B. C. We spent 13 days on water and in spite of the stormy weather we arrived ahead of schedule, always making more than 16 mph. It took us nine hours of traveling between Seattle and Vancouver. In spite of the stormy weather we arrived in the Yokohama three days ahead of schedule. This made our stay in Yokohama six days. We were disappointed in not being met by the missionaries we were expecting to see, but found out later they were a day late in getting to the boat and the letter was not delivered to us till too late for us to get in touch with them.

The mosquito nets over the beds here are something new to us. They are fastened to the ceiling and extend from the floor to about two feet from the ceiling. They are about 15 yards around and when spread resembles umbrellas. This net is very finely woven and is all in one piece.

The kiddies are spending most of their time outside watching the boats and fishermen. I spend most of mine here in the hotel room doing the little things that a mother of five needs to do and then

14

the writing. Since we are to pay for room and board, we are glad to know how to get along with as little as possible. Sightseeing cost too much for faith missionaries but there is a park nearby and the children have been there and also to the swimming pool.

They sing every chance they get. At the pool the lady caretaker and about 300 children just about crowded them out. Many people have stopped Alfred and marveled over five kiddies.

The weather has been very hot in Japan. You just cook, washed up to keep feeling clean and then you cook all over again. The shower did not cool very much.

We do have much to praise the Lord for and pray God to bless the dear ones in America.

On-board the Terukuni Maru

God bless you all. I feel I must drop you a line before the boat pulls out this afternoon. I have not been able to write much lately. The weather is hot and stuffy and I have not had a very good place to put my machine for writing. The dining room is hot and the smoking room tables are all filled up with men filling out freight billings. Today I have ventured on forbidden territory, second-class room for writing.

They seem to be more particular on this boat as to where the different classes sit. Our cabin room is large and roomy but it is way, way down.

We have been docked here since Monday evening (this was written from Kobe, Japan September 4th). We have only traveled 34 hours since we left Yokohama, Aug. 29. The rest of the time has been spent in stopping and loading up freight.

I would advise anyone else coming to have it understood with the steamship company that after you reach Yokohama or Kobe, you might choose the first possible boat to take you onto your destination. In this way you can save time. Had we known this, we could have taken a French boat direct to Haiphong without these long stopovers and still there would be enough stops to take care of business matters on the way. We find you can buy a straight ticket from one end of the world to the other and stop when and where you want to.

We have met some missionaries on-board who are going to Korea. They are not Pentecostal and the lady was shocked beyond words because we had never been vaccinated and was surprised that we were even allowed to enter Japan without several shots of vaccine. Then our being out with five children—why their mission board would not think of sending anyone out with more than one. Well, we praise the Lord that it is He that is sending us and not a mission board and that we look to God for our health and our support.

• CHAPTER 4 •

Hong Kong

September 10, 1936

Dear ones in Spokane and America,

Praise the Lord from whom all blessings flow. We are nearly 5,881 miles from Vancouver B. C. The Lord has been with us, so that it doesn't seem as far to us as it may to some of you. He has made the trip very easy for us in a great many ways. Just today I found out that there is much complaining about the service that people received in the higher class part of the ship, so I am glad that we traveled third class.

Of course, you will want to know about the health of the children, as, when I wrote last, I requested prayer for Ruth and David. Well God is the healer. I felt at the time, in the spirit, that they were suffering from malaria fever, but I did not tell even Alfred about it. Mark also took sick. Ruth seemed to suffer the most and as she had a cold along with it. One evening when I was visiting with a lady, and she told me the symptoms of malaria, and by what she told me, I knew that Mark, David and Ruth had it. But praise the Lord! They are all well at this time.

Please continue to hold us up in prayer as we travel on. I can almost see you all as your prayers follow us up, and it makes my heart rejoice.

Praise the Lord for his goodness! Hallelujah! I know that nothing shall befall us that is not in His plan.

The weather has been slightly cooler, and today we had a shower of rain. We hear all sorts of weather predictions. Some say it will be cooler, but the majority predicts hot weather.

September 11, 1936—Praise the Lord, we are now in Hong Kong. Our ship arrived in town late the evening of the tenth; Brother Bullock was there to meet us, but we stayed on the boat until today the 11th, because the youngsters were in bed already. The Bullets have a lovely place. I am now there. We have met the students of the Bible school, and it was a real joy to hear them sing with shining faces some of the same songs we sing at home. We leave tomorrow on the next boat to Hiaphong.

No money has been given us since we left. The two-day trip to Hiaphong is costing us $107.60 American money. We don't know yet what the train fare will be from there to Yunnan Fu, but at the rate things are going, I guess we will be broke when we get there. But, praise the Lord! We know He is able to keep that which we have committed unto him.

Greetings to all the saints. I hope you are all fat in the spirit, as Alfred says.

Lots of love,
Mrs. A.M. Bernheim and family

• CHAPTER 5 •

December 12, 1936

Dear ones at home in America:

Praise God from whom all blessings flow.

We are at this time praising God for his wonderful deliverance from death, as Alfred and I have both been near death in the last few weeks. Before we took sick, the Lord gave Alfred a dream of warning that we did not fully understand at the time, showing that we had survived a very serious case of poisoning.

Alfred was the first to take sick, but as it did not develop so strongly until a few days later, we thought we had the victory. I took sick very suddenly after a prayer meeting. I certainly did suffer; I had six sinking spells, similar to fainting, although different and rather unexplainable. Alfred was sick at the same time, but for a week or more after I was in bed he struggled hard to keep on his feet for someone had to take care of the children. At last his strength gave out and had to go to bed. Even before he went to bed, he would be walking across the room and suddenly dropped to the floor in a faint. Because he fought so hard to stay up, it is taking him longer to get on his feet again, but God has wonderfully undertaken and he is gaining strength every day.

The other missionaries in the city were very kind to us during our affliction. We do praise the Lord for this. When we could not get up, some of them would bring us our breakfast, and others would come and cook a meal for the children and us. They brought us good bread and fruit to strengthen our weak bodies. We have been trying to live on Chinese food as cheaply as possible, but our bodies are not yet accustomed to such a sudden change, so from now on, we will have to buy food more suited to our needs.

We certainly do need your prayers. Other missionaries tell us that from now until the end of March is the dry season when the air is full of germs of unspeakable sicknesses and a newcomer, especially, is very subject to disease. Our trust is in the living God.

As far as we can see at present, many Pentecostal missionaries in China have compromised greatly on divine healing. "That is all right in America", they say, "where all the surroundings are sanitary, but China knows nothing of sanitation, so we must take this and that to prevent infection, and the first thing to do is to call a doctor."

I am still persuaded, as I have written before, that nothing shall befall us that is not in God's plan. Alfred says that it is too late now to turn from trusting the Lord, as we have proved Him all sufficient for the last 13 years and we are both persuaded that God is just as big in China as He is in Spokane.

Esther, also, was sick, but she seems to be all right now. Mark has been sick, too, the last few days, and still is not quite himself, but hates to stay in bed. None of us have escaped the testing, but we know that if we prove true, we shall come forth as pure gold.

Alfred's plans, which are somewhat upset by his illness, were to go out to the country places around with gospels and tracts. A young Chinese evangelist will accompany him, leading as soon as he is strong enough. Perhaps by the time you get this letter, he will be in the mountains, as he planned. The robbers section is only eight days journey from here. In one section, the robbers went to the town, burning the houses and capturing and carrying off whom they would, then proceeding on to the next town.

We know you will continue to pray for us, as that is your part in this great missionary work.

Yours for souls in China,
The Bernheim family
LIFE IN YUNNAN FU

Excerpts from recent Bernheim letters

I remember saying once that sometime I would tell you about housekeeping in China. The kitchen has a brick stove in it about table height with a hole that you cook on. Charcoal is used for fuel. The fire is started with a little pitch and kindling and the charcoal put on top, then you have to fan and fan the fire with a big fan until the charcoal gets red hot. Every time you have to fan the fires, ashes fly all over everything in the kitchen, so you soon eat a peck of ashes with everything you cooked.

Because the fumes from the charcoal are very bad and it is so easy to become poisoned from them, it is necessary to have lots of fresh (if it can be called *fresh* in this country where it is so full of odors) air in the room or else to keep a pan of water boiling to supply fresh oxygen.

Cooking is quite a problem, as you can cook only one kettle at a time unless you have an extra fire pot, so if you prepare several dishes, the first one must be we reheated or else eaten cold.

Most foreigners have a cook that they keep busy cooking their food from morning till night. As using my pressure cooker save lots of time, I do the cooking myself. One thing is certain about doing the cooking myself, should I cook chicken; I know very well who eats the broth. One of our neighbors complained that when the cook cooks a chicken, he drinks the broth and pours hot water on for them.

Every drop of water for drinking and eating in this country has to be boiled first because of impurities. We keep a jug for drinking that has to be freshly boiled every day.

The children are trying to do school lessons and to learn Chinese. A young Chinese evangelist comes to teach us. We have to repeat the words over and over until we get just the correct sound, because just a slight raising or lowering of your voice makes the word means something entirely different. You must say the middle or the last of the sentence first.

We see many things in China that would seem very queer to you dear one at home. It is very common to see a man walking down the street with a string of fire crackers about four feet long, going off from the bottom to the top. This, we are told, it is the sign that someone has died. Sometimes the funeral possession follows immediately, and sometimes the firecrackers are shot off immediately after the death.

In order to save feeding the calves, they kill them and stuff the skin with straw. This stuffed skin is carried around for the cow to smell and lick and that is how she stays a contented cow. Alfred was told about this custom, and then the other day he saw a man carrying a stuffed calf down the street with the old cow following. When the man stopped, the cow smelled the calf and all was well.

The man with the cow was doing his shopping. You can shop from early-morning till midnight. Almost everything is sold on the street. Sometimes the seller runs up-and-down the street calling out the names of his wares, even at all hours of the night.

• CHAPTER 6 •

Kunming, Yunnan Province. S.W. China

December 22nd, 1936

Dear one in the Lord,

We are still praising the Lord "through it all". Alfred is getting stronger every day, although he has not been able to venture out yet. He is saving his strength for a trip to the country that he plans on making, Lord willing, in the future. I have gained strength so that I really feel quite well, although I know that I am not fully strong yet. We do praise the Lord for his love and mercy to us.

Saturday I took the children to a program given not far from where we live, by a German sister, who has a rescue home for slave girls. The whole program was given by the little slave girls, who quoted scripture in Chinese, and put on a touching little play about a little girl's generosity in giving her clothes to the poor till she was left destitute, but finally was abundantly rewarded for kindness to the poor and needy.

Many of the slave girls are feeble minded, because they are so abused by their masters. In the sisters home they are happy and well cared for. It cost about two dollars in gold to feed the slave girls a month in this rescue home. Many other girls have been bought by foreigners, and placed there in her care.

I expect, Lord willing, to visit the slave prison near us soon, and when I do, I will tell you all about it. The girls are not put in the prison because of any crime they have committed, but because their masters have discarded them there. Should a man's wife die, he could go to this prison, buy a slave, and do as he pleases with her. No wonder so many of the poor girls are feeble minded! It is really a miracle that many of them can learn anything considering the treatment they have undergone.

Oh how it makes my heart ache to do more for the Lord! We witness to all that we meet, giving out all that we have learned, and trust in God to water the seed that it may bring forth fruit in the harvest. We have prayer meetings here in our home attended by those of different nationalities, and in that way we are keeping the home fires burning.

Thank you for the offering you sent us, and may the Lord reward you all.

This is the first Christmas that our children will be without a Christmas tree. But to make things look cheery, we have made some white paper flowers trimmed in red. Of course, Esther had a hand in it.

Mark wishes he had a nice red apple, and so does Alfred. That is one of the things we miss that cannot be gotten here. Of course, that is not the only thing, but we do not look to that, as we are happy to know we are where the Lord has need of us.

We see wonderful opportunities in the near future. We hear that there are places in the mountains that are open for the gospel were there are no missionaries. These places are hard and dangerous, but we feel led to move on, where no one else is willing to go, as the Lord leads. We covet your prayers in this behalf most earnestly.

The kiddies are learning the Chinese language rapidly, and are able to understand ever so much more. Usually, what one doesn't know another does, so we get along quite well with the language. Even I can make myself understood.

The children seem to be well now. The baby is just three months old, smiling and happy, a very good little girl. I think she will be like Esther. [Lois was born after they arrived in China].

We are rejoicing in the way the Lord has taking care of us. "God is good" even in China.

Christian love to all,
Yours in the master service,
The Bernheim family

• CHAPTER 7 •

January 10, 1937

To All the Loved Ones at Home,

Praise the Lord for His love to us! That is ever a new story as we think of His mercy to us who are witnesses for Him alive because He healed us.

Our mail is very often delayed, to be delivered whenever they please. The recent three day New Year celebration was the cause of some of our mail being delayed. The main Chinese General is a Christian and has ordered China to keep the New Year on January 1st. There were also a number of political festivities at that time to celebrate his release from capture, a time of great joy in China and much commotion.

In just a month from now the old Chinese New Year will be celebrated, the festivities and idol worship connected with it lasting, we are told, two weeks.

I know you will be interested in hearing about our Christmas. Some missionaries here invited us all over for supper and a Christmas tree the evening of the 23rd. Alfred was not well enough to go, so Ruth stayed home with him. We had a lovely chicken supper. There were gifts for all the kiddies, and everyone spent an enjoyable evening singing carols.

Becky Croasmun

Our Christmas dinner at home on the 25th consisted of some potatoes that were green, Chinese carrots, and goat meat. We were glad and thankful that we're all well enough to eat it. Beef meat is expensive, and, although lots of people turn their nose at goat meat, it seems to suit our purse better.

On the 29th, another foreign family invited the kiddies for a Christmas tree, treat and refreshments.

About the greatest excitement of Christmas week was a mother's giving away her 3 daughters, two of them to a slave home. As the slave home does not take babies, she intended to throw the 2 month old baby to the dogs, but another missionary heard of it and adopted the baby. We have heard that two baby girls were thrown to the dogs not far from our home. Oh, how it makes our hearts ache, and long more and more earnestly to be able to tell them about Jesus! We feel that we can never do enough for all that God has done for us.

We all continue to learn more of the language, both in speaking and understanding it. The children, especially, are learning fast.

Our little Lois Margaret tries so hard to sit up; she hates to have her head down on the pillow, but wants it up so that she can see everything around. She topples backward and rolls over when trying to sit up, but makes a great effort to lift her head high again. I don't know just what she weighs as we have no scale. She felt fine even when I was so very sick; a thing that I feel was a real miracle.

I am sure the weather here would be of interest to you. When the sun shines, it is warm in the sun but cold in the house between the mud walls. At night we have quite a heavy frost, and there was a little snow one day.

It is quite windy and the air is full of disease germs. The smell from the open sewage is quite enough to spoil your appetite when you are eating. Yet, by the grace of God, it is possible to eat a hearty meal as the Lord provides it.

We can't do much baking here as our oven is just an oil tin. The flour isn't good for much; it is soggy no matter what I do, and very wormy.

It is a battle to try to get clean things to eat in this country. Everything we buy is sold on the street, and is very dirty, often filthy, so that it must be washed and boiled before being used. Meat often looks as if it had been dipped in *dung*. The sugar that we buy is brown and is sold in chunks so that we do not see the dirt, but when we boil it into syrup we can see the dirt we have been eating as it stays in the bottom of the pan or else forms a scum on top. Some expensive white sugar was given us for Christmas, but as we dipped some out for our tea, we could see that it was full of hair, and when we melted it, oh my, you should have see the dirt. The native flour is full of worms, some of them an inch long, some so small that they go through the sifter. The Chinese say, "Cook em, kill em, everything", and we have to eat. So we pray that the Lord will give us a missionary stomach to digest all these things.

The water also is very impure. A missionary from a mountain village called on us a few days ago, and told of a man overtaken by thirst, which, seeing a stream of water falling from a mountain drank of that water, and his body immediately beginning to bloat, in a few minutes he dropped dead. Not a drop of water can be used that has not first been boiled.

• CHAPTER 8 •

January 11, 1937

This has been a great day. A young Chinese Christian is very friendly toward us, saying that he likes us because we do not hold ourselves higher than the Chinese people. He greatly desires to fellowship with us, that he may *pattern after* us.

Today he wanted to show his friendship by bringing us a Chinese feast. He brought a duck, cooked, but not done enough for us to really enjoy it; spiced roast beef, cold and underdone; dried beef, hard, hot, seasoned with red pepper, onions, brown sugar, and vinegar; fried fish, seasoned with ginger; some kind of sausage which might have been good had the casing been thoroughly washed before stuffing; cabbage cooked rare, highly seasoned with salt; a savory soup which the youngsters declare, was made of the entrails of the duck; thin fried goat cheese; fried walnuts; sweet steamed biscuits or dumplings; and thin slices of mutton. After the meal, we all enjoyed a few cups of tea which I served. In all, it would have been a delicious meal had it been really cleaned, cooked properly, and seasoned with a little less red pepper. But praise the Lord; we had a happy time together. As he says, "We are in Jesus." We had prayer together with the Chinese friends that he brought.

Last week our hearts were made to rejoice as two Chinese men that we have talked to a number of times presented us with a basket of eggs. It has been said that you never can get anything out of the Chinese, and they always take from you all that they possibly can, but when we offered to pay for the eggs, they flatly refused to let us, saying that it was their pleasure. So we thank God for having touched their hearts, and we pray that the seed that is sown may grow.

I was quite amused the other day. You see, I have not been out a great deal in the strange parts of the town, but the other day when I was farther from home than usual, the people noticed that I was a stranger and I heard them saying, *baa some moo*. I looked around to see who was speaking to me, as our Chinese name is *baa* meaning *white*, and *some moo* means a married lady teacher. When I saw no one that I knew, then I realized that they had me spotted as a new foreigner. The Chinese cannot pronounce American names as we do, so immediately they give you one that they can speak.

A robber visited us this morning. He did no damage to our property, and we hope to see him saved some day.

I hope that the letters that were addressed to Kunming arrive all right. We are now instructed to add *Yunnanfu* in parentheses after the word Kunming.

We still need your prayers in every way. Ruth has a bad cold, Alfred (Max) is recovering, praise the Lord, and the rest seem quite well.

Yours in His service,
The Bernheim Family

• CHAPTER 9 •

Dear loved ones at home,

Peace to you. God bless you everyone.

Mr. Bernheim has recently returned from an evangelist trip into the country with a young Chinese Christian. The first 15 miles of the trip was through well-populated country where they were kept very busy giving tracts and portions of scripture to all that they met. They saw many people going for miles and miles carrying heavy loads on their backs. Some carried rice that they were taking to town to sell, others had loads of water brush and rice straw, others were carrying charcoal, and a few carried loads of wood although wood is very scarce. They saw horses and donkeys very heavily loaded as the people seem to have no idea how heavy a load an animal should carry. For several miles they were walking past fields where vegetables are raise, and they saw many water buffalo's working in them. The odor from these fields was most sickening because they were fertilized by the city sewage.

When they reached a village they went into the gardens surrounding the temple. To the many people that had been worshiping the idols of the temple they witnessed the saving power of our Lord Jesus Christ, giving them portions of God's word. The people listened with attentive ears.

After leaving this village, they soon reached the mountains. They could not afford to hire donkeys or carriers, so must climb the mountains on foot. Some places in the winding trails were so steep that they almost slipped backwards, as their feet were not as nimble as those of the donkeys that they were continually meeting on the road. The donkey drivers and all the others they met during the trip heard the gospel message before they were allowed to pass.

Finally they reached another large temple filled with idols of all kinds. Here they were dealing with the tribal people rather than the Chinese, although they spoke the Chinese language. A number of the Chinese lamas in the temple listened to them with a very eager expressions as they told of the one true and living God who is very powerful. The lamas invited them to have tea, and as they were tired and hungry, they accepted the invitation gratefully, and used that opportunity to tell them that their idols were the work a man, and not of God.

Alfred has not been very strong since his illness, so he perspired greatly from weakness as he climbed the stony paths, but the joy of the Lord strengthened his body so that he was able each day to go on until the Lord bade them rest when their days labor ended. Day by day he grew stronger, and his soul was made to rejoice as he gave forth God's word.

As Mr. Bernheim and his Chinese companion traveled on through the mountains, they lost their way and many times did not know what direction to go, yet God so guided their steps that they met many people that needed the gospel message and eventually they found a main trail again. The Lord must have been guiding them, because they reach their destination on market day when the village was crowded with people who had gathered to buy and sell and exchange their commodities, and they had a wonderful opportunity to witness to all these of the saving power of Christ. Soldiers guarded the village, as robbers were numerous. The gospel message was given to several who appeared to be robbers. Feeling the hand of God upon them, Alfred and his companion had no fear.

We feel that the Lord will greatly bless the seed that has been sown. Although in this world we may not see all that God does, yet when he gives us our rewards, we shall know what He had accomplished.

Yours for souls,
Emily Bernheim

• CHAPTER 10 •

February 10, 1937

Dear friends,

We do thank the Lord and all of you, too, for the money sent to us. We are living as cheaply as possible, our food is meat, small potatoes that are nearly always green, a few Chinese vegetables—the carrots and spinach are quite good—and wheat and corn that we buy and grind ourselves for breakfast food. None of these have the strength that food at home does. Often one still feels hungry after eating all that is possible. That seems queer, I know but it is so.

Prices are very high due to the lack of rain. Many things cost twice what they did last fall. But we are looking to the Lord to supply for us according to his will.

We feel that God is working because the devil is hard on our trail. One day a wall fell in just a few feet from where Esther and I were walking, God protected as from injury, Praise His name.

Another time I was going to a prayer meeting when a dog, coming up from behind me, bit me three times through my clothes into my flesh. Although I expected the Lord will have healed it before you get this letter, please remember me and all of us in prayer.

Smallpox is very bad this year. In one town over 100 children died from the disease this winter. The chief cause is the lack of rain. The whirlwinds carry the germs all over.

There is no isolation of the sick ones; they walk the streets with all their marks exposed if they are at all able. Mothers carry their sick babies around on their backs and beg, telling you all about the sick child and showing you the sores to arouse your sympathy. Many people torture themselves making sores on their legs and are continually digging at them in order to show you their misery so that they will have cause to beg. Oh, how our hearts ache as we see all this!

Many are blind. These touch one's heart the most. There is a school for blind girls here run by some German sisters. The C.I.M. are planning to open one for the boys soon. Many will never consent to go to these schools as they get more by begging than they could otherwise make. Those who own the beggars use them as a tool to get some easy money. Oh how we need prayer that God will protect and deliver us as we mingle with all the suffering and disease!

The Chinese New Year started February 11th, and all China has on its best. No work was done today and everything will be closed for two weeks. Although the national government is counting January 1st as the New Year, Yunnan province is a rebel and observes the old custom. Many have bought new clothes for the occasion; shops have red mottos hanging over them with big black Chinese characters painted on them; rice balls as big as basketballs have been sold for the last two weeks in honor of the occasion; and all sorts of weird lanterns and paper dangles are to be seen everywhere.

Yours in His glad service,
Emily Bernheim

• CHAPTER II •

April 4, 1937

Dear ones in the homeland,

"Praise ye the Lord, Praise, oh, ye servants of the Lord, praise the name of the Lord." Psalms 113:1. "Who is like unto the Lord our God, who dwells on high, who humbles Himself to behold the things that are in Heaven and in the earth?" Psalms 113: 5, 6.

Yes, we are praising the Lord for much these days, for the things that He has been mindful of, for us, and we also praise the Lord for what He will do, although it is unseen at present. God knows all things beforehand; therefore, we give Him praise. As we look around us, we can see the touch of His hand.

Two weeks ago we received orders that we would have to find another house, because our landlady wanted the house we were living in for members of her own family. Houses to live in are a rare thing, and we were told by others that have been looking for houses that there was not a vacant house in the town. We were both sick when we were told to move, so God, who knows all things, was told about our need. Of course He knew it first, but as we told Him all about the matter in prayer, we received the answer that He had a place for us. So, according to His Word He has given us a suitable place of abode for the present.

It is not a house like you might imagine, but, for us, it does very well indeed. It is half a house, with the landlady living in the other half.

Our living apartment consists of two upstairs rooms and two downstairs rooms. The roof extending about nine feet out from the rooms is made of hard baked tile that would be in good shape except that the robbers have crawled over them so much that the tiles are all out of place. We are praying that the Lord will keep out the robbers, as well as the rain that is now beginning to come. Just a few nights ago, the robbers visited a place not far from here but were frightened away. The way the houses are built they can walk from one roof to another in every direction without having to drop to the ground. From one shed roof they could step right into our upper rooms, but we leave it all in God's hands, as we know He will care for as with His angels while we sleep.

The walls are made of mud. The windows are shut out with boards. Very fortunately the house has a board floor; usually the floors are made of mud, too. The rats have made many instances into the house and make themselves quite at home. I haven't been able to find out for certain if the rats are used for food when they are caught or not, but I know they are sometimes carried through the street as if they were prized very highly. All entrails are used for food. When we were so ill recently, we bought a chicken so we could have a nice broth, and our wash lady, seeing that I did not want the entrails, asked if she could have them. She thanked me most heartily for them and fixed a real feast out of them for herself. Nothing is wasted in this country.

Our beds have been loaned to us. They are made of bamboo straw over two-by-fours, and set across wooden horses to keep them off the floor. Praise the Lord; they are better than just boards. This house has some chairs in it. They are very antique and ancient, and so heavy that if the children want to move them, they have to drag them across the floor, but they are quite comfortable to sit on, at least, for missionaries. There is also a writing table in the house that falls into three pieces when it is moved. We found that out when we washed the floor, but when all in one-piece, it is quite convenient. We have small fire pots to cook on made of clay. We have no stove, as the only stove is the other part of the house.

This has been a long dry season with no rain. The lama priests tell the people that it is because the white people have come to the country that they have no rain. One missionary who has been here for about 15 years says that when such conditions prevail, it is very dangerous for a white person to show himself on the street, that they will surely try to kill you with their hidden knives. We have no fear, because we feel the steps of the righteous are *ordered by the Lord.*

Today it is raining. We are thankful, as we have been asking the Lord to send the rain in His time, that the spread of the gospel be not hindered. At the same time was it not good of the Lord to help us to move before it did rain? Praise His name.

We formally lived at the north end of town and are now living at the west end, so we have a new district in which to witness for the Lord. Yesterday a lady was coming down the street yelling, "Eggs to sell, eggs, eggs!" Before I had my eggs safely in my bowl,

I was surrounded by 30 people, old and young. I told them all I could about my precious Savior. My wash lady is always coming to my rescue when I have difficulty making myself understood. She helped me bargained for the eggs, and then she helped me tell them about the Jesus that loves the Chinese, too. Several times yesterday the doorway was crowded with people wanting to see just what we are like. One little girl said, "See that baby, it is beautiful!" She, herself, was a sweet little lady, so I quickly said, "You are beautiful too." She was so surprised that she hid herself between the others. She had not heard a white lady speak her language, so she did not know what to think about it, and then, perhaps, no one had ever told her that she was nice looking.

The month of March proved very trying to our health. Although we were tested severely, God was present to heal us. While I was suffering, God gave me the Ninety-first Psalm and revealed that, although we are very weak now in many ways, yet at the same time He is strengthening our bodies through these sicknesses that we may be able to resist and be immune to the plagues that prevail on every hand. So we say *amen* to the Lord and to His will. God has given us the strengths to move. Although we feel very weak, yet we know that He is preparing our bodies for other work. So our hearts are filled with praise, as we know our God doeth with all things well. Many have died in recent weeks. Just a few days ago, four funeral processions passed in a very few minutes. We thank you all for your prayers as we continue to hold up the bloodstained banner to those who do not know Him.

We have had some trouble in receiving letters from home, so we would advise those wishing to send funds for the work here to please send them to the Philadelphian Church office; they will know best how to take care of them so they will reach their destination safely. We have found out that mail robbers are not scarce in China. One missionary almost starved because his mail was robbed. He, with his wife and baby, escaped from a mountain town just skin and bone. God, in mercy, restored them to health again. This shows the power of God, as they had been sick unto death from the lack of food.

Not long ago we were told that in a village not so far from here a mother gave birth to five baby girls all living, but the relatives decided that the best thing to do was to throw them away. Oh, that we could only rescue all these for the Lord! The sad part of it is that we hear of them after it has happened. But we feel that when the gospel reaches their hearts, the girls will be as welcomed as the boys. So don't forget to pray for us and the work here.

We praise God for the young people who answer the call of God to carry the gospel to foreign fields. At the same time, I would plead with the young men that they also let God lead them into the harvest field, as we notice that it is mostly the women who have been willing to bring the gospel to the heathen, the men being scarce in this field. One English girl here in the city now was in the hospital for 16 weeks and near death many times, as she had to flee from the Reds and was without food and water for days till her tongue was swollen and hanging from her mouth. Several girls have lost their co-workers from the disease and sickness that rages through the land, but the gospel must go forth. When one girl was rebuked for preaching the gospel, she said that the reason she came was because some man had said "No" to God, and God, seeing her in the kitchen, asked her if she would go, and she said "Yes, Lord." We have been rebuked for coming to China with a family and on faith, but perhaps some couples without children and with good backing refused to go. We are glad that we're willing to say, "yes, Lord."

Some of us missionaries are planning, Lord willing, to meet together at least once a week to have a day of fasting and prayer for a Holy Ghost revival in China, and also that God will pour out His Spirit on the missionaries in the various fields, and will remove those that are not in His will or else bring them into His will. It is only through prayer that a revival can come. We need your help in this prayer request, and you, too, will receive your share of the blessing.

In our new place of abode, we are getting more and more opportunity to witness for the Lord. It has taken many attempts to write this letter, as the Chinese keep coming in continually. I cannot tell you how many have been witnessed to today. Pray that the Lord will water the seed and let it bring forth fruit. The darkness that reigns in our hearts cannot be described on paper. But pray, Pray, PRAY! God is stronger than the devil.

Yours in his service,
The Bernheim family

• CHAPTER 12 •

Chinese baby adopted by Bernheim's

Mrs. Bernheim describes visit to slave prison

April 17, 1937

Dear Ones in the Lord,

Greetings to you all in the name of our precious Lord and Savior.

When I last wrote to you, I gave our address as No. 13, but this week all the street numbers have been changed and our lot fell to No. 7. We feel that there is something significant about this address *Ping An Kai* means *Peace Street,* and seven is the perfect number, so Praise God, we know this is the place He has for us at this time.

We live now at the southwest edge of town, about seven houses from the end, so we can look over the roofs from our bedrooms and see the wall. The town is surrounded by a great wall having gates at the north, south, east and west sides, which are closed in times of war and trouble in order to protect the city.

The sun is beginning to be very warm now. If the sun strikes you even at 6 a.m., you feel sick and faint, so we start our day early and keep out of the sun as much as possible. Ruth and David have been sick the last few days. I believe it was caused by the rays of the sun.

Another bad epidemic that of spinal meningitis, is raging through the nation. One hospital has 500 cases, another 200, and many others scattered throughout the town. We are trusting in the true and living God to bring us safely through and to protect us with His precious blood. The foreigners get blamed for this plague, just as with the dry season. One can feel their staring eyes when walking through the streets and can hear their darkening hearts blaming us for the disaster. Yet our hearts go out to them in love and longing, that they might know our Jesus, too.

Not long ago I had an opportunity to visit the slave prison. It was a pitiful site indeed. About 30 of the inmates, each holding her rice bowl in her hand, were gathered in a shed for Gospel service. Many were feeble minded from the abuse of masters and are now cast off and in this prison awaiting new masters or death. They are kept with the women criminal prisoners, so it is not long until the minds are filled with all manner of sin and thoughts of vice. Most of them listened attentively to the gospel message that went forth and they all joined in the songs and prayer. Several insane women were making screeching noises and attracting the attention of as many as possible, but I prayed that the Lord to keep them all peaceful during the service. After the service each one was given a portion of food, a treat they always look forward to, as they get very little to eat otherwise. That is one reason that they often take sick and die while in the prison. I went to their sleeping room, which is where the chickens were kept. A thin worn-out straw rug on a few boards laid across wooden horses with no covering or pillow or anything like that was the bed.

On this they huddled together to keep warm in the wintertime. In the summer I am sure they must smother, or else sleep on the dirt floor. One room was confined to the opium smokers and what a horrid looking place it was! The filthiest people in America cannot even imagine what filth is as we see it here! Pray that the gospel may reach these poor souls and they may accept Jesus as the Savior.

In regard to sending us clothing and supplies from America, I don't think it pays to send anything such a long distance. We have three taxes to pay on packages, first, a postage tax, second, a custom tax, and third, a luxury tax. Custom and luxury taxes are charged according to the contents of the package and the mood of the man in charge, which often is not very pleasant because they do not like imported packages. Because of this, one is often forced to spend a lot of money that would otherwise be used differently before getting a package from the post office. One missionary here received a box of chocolates and had to pay seven dollars American money before taking them home.

It would not be advisable to send clothing, as the winter vary so much that what we are wearing now will not do in a month or two. There really is no comparison between the weather here and in America. Then the children have grown so much that unless I sent the measurements for clothes, they would not fit, and probably by the time the things arrive, they would not fit anyway.

If people want to help, let them give Mrs. Watson the money to send us, and we can use it here for what is needed most. If someone still wants to send something please heed the following instructions: do not have the clothing iron or pack fancy: it is better to have it starched, wrinkled, and not ironed. A few pieces of old clothing will make the rate cheaper at this end, but if it is not very wearable, it would not pay send it. Mark the packages "no commercial value," or "value not more than $.99." Be sure it contains no silk, as that is taxed very high. The things should look old and wrinkled when they get here. We have learned this through conversation with other missionaries. Many of them are disgusted with receiving packages, but hate to tell people not to send them. Finally, everyone that sends a package should also send an offering of at least five dollars to help take care of the customs, or would not be fair to us.

April 25, 1937

This has been such a wonderful week that we must let you know about it. Monday the Lord gave us the 121st Psalm and we were meditating especially on the third and fourth verse: "He will not suffer thy foot to be moved; He that keepeth thee will not slumber. Behold, He that keepeth Israel shall neither slumber nor sleep." We went to bed rather tired, but just when we naturally would be sleeping the most soundly, the Lord suddenly woke Alfred, telling him to go look out of the window. There in the darkness on the wall of our backyard, he saw a man crawling. When the intruder was almost ready to approach the porch door to our own rooms, Alfred suddenly flash the light in his face. He flashed his light and Alfred very silently in exchange then he turned and slowly crawled away. Alfred called me and together we watched him as the prowled around the neighborhood on the roofs of all the houses, flashing his light into the different yards looking around. Just that day the Lord had told Alfred to buy a

Becky Croasmun

battery for the flashlight. Praise the Lord, for being mindful for us and not slumbering or being asleep when we needed Him. That is always the way, He is there just when needed most.

The next news item of the week is the new baby girl which was rescued and given to us. Praise the Lord! This is one that the dogs are not going to eat. It looks as if it had been badly abused; its little body is black a blue in many places. She is so thin and starved that she hardly knows what to do when she has the bottle in her mouth, although she is learning to take it. She has a very bad cold on her chest, so please remember her in prayer that her little life may be the means of salvation to someone.

Today two high-class women came to the house. They told me that Lois was a very pretty baby, but that the Chinese baby was no good, as she was a girl and so very small. I told them that Jesus loved the little girls, and after she had enough milk, she, too, would be fat like our little Lois Margaret. The Lord helped me and I was able to talk quite a bit to these women. They understood all that I said and marveled at my being able to speak their language when I had been there such a short time.

Alfred is feeling well again and is gaining strength. I, too, am feeling quite as well as usual.

Yours for souls,
The Bernheim family,
Emily Bernheim

• CHAPTER 13 •

Brother Bernheim's Testimony

God says, "In everything give thanks," and "all things work together for good to those who love God and are called according to his purpose." I am considering this test of malaria, as one of "all things," and am praising the Lord for His love goodness to me. In the natural, my case would have been almost unbearable, but, Praise God! We are not living in the natural, but in the supernatural, living in the Spirit and close to God, under the precious blood of Jesus.

It is almost impossible to describe it on paper. I had a very high temperature. Fever and chills were raging in my body at the same time. My face was purple with the fever. I would doze off to sleep in this feverish condition, and finding it impossible to breathe through my nose, would gasp for breath with my mouth open. The fever so parched my tongue and throat that it was impossible to swallow water when I awoke. My tongue cracked in two places, which was very painful. Esther would pour water and milk in my mouth with a teaspoon to quench my thirst and soak my parched throat, as I was too helpless to move to take a drink myself.

With a cracked tongue, my speech was hindered, but I could still talk to God. Praise the Lord! With Him my speech was unhindered. He always talked to me. Many times when I thought I was gasping my last breath, I heard the voice of my beloved say "I am your present help in the time the need". My faith grew by leaps and bounds as I reviewed many instances in my past life when Jesus, my Savior and Redeemer, had protected and healed me and delivered me from death.

There was the time when, driving my first car in Chicago, I ran in between two elevated train post. The car was a total wreck, but God delivered me without a scratch. And then, was He not with me, in my sleep; I went off a mountain in California driving a five-ton white truck? Did he not heal my body that was crippled as a result that accident? Did he not protect all our lives in the gospel car many times, sparing us from tipping over many grades, and taking us safely over many unseen curves? One particular instance came to my mind especially. I glanced off the road to see some scenery and the gospel car swerved off the curve, but God took us safely down the bank and had a flat place prepared so we could easily get back to the highway again.

Did not God spare my life when five bandits robbed the mail in the post office in Los Angeles? They had bound and gagged me. Their guns were cocked ready to force me into the eternity, but God stayed their wicked hands. And many other things did I review, as I lay there, with praise and thanksgiving that I was trusting in such a wonderful Savior.

As I look to Jesus and the cross where He died for me, I see the power of His resurrection. That same power is able to deliver me now from the chills and fever that rage in this body of clay. I know I am in His keeping, but I want to be a yielded vessel that He may be glorified, no matter what should befall me. It is not mine to question, "Why should this be?" For lo! He doeth all things well. I just say, "Amen, Lord, have thine own way". By faith we see the victory ahead. That is one thing the devil can't take from us: he is a defeated foe—Jesus is our victory

Alfred Max Bernheim

• CHAPTER 14 •

Kunming, Yunnanfu

May 13, 1937

Dear Ones at home,

Praise God from whom all blessing flow. The last few weeks have been busy ones, and we praise the Lord for the work that He gives us to do. The Lord has taken home to Himself the little Chinese baby that He gave us, so she will no longer suffer. As I wrote before, she was very sick and had been badly abused so that her little body was black and blue. We feel that it was best that God took her away, and we give Him thanks in all things.

All of our children have been suffering in health in various ways since we wrote last, but, thank God, He has been with us to deliver. We are so glad that we can trust Him for our health.

It is getting very warm and the mosquitoes are beginning to come. I have made mosquitoes nets for the beds. They serve a double purpose as they also keep the rats off the bed.

We have had a few days of nice rain. We thank the Lord for that. A good rainy season will give rice to the Chinese and reduce sickness in general. You at home cannot conceive the thought of all the germs that go through the air in dry weather. Although, we see that sanitary conditions are improving to the public eye, yet what is hidden behind the walls is unspeakable.

The Lord is with us and is honoring our testimony for Him in this neighborhood. There is a soldier who often visits the adjoining house. His great delight is to come over and talk to the children, and they enjoy singing to him and telling him the story of Jesus. Since they have been talking to him, he has bought a testament. At first he smoked cigarettes, but one day the children told him that cigarettes were bad. When he wanted to know if *Jesus people* smoked, we explained to him the harm that comes from tobacco. He had four cigarettes in his pocket, which he immediately took out and put into the fire. Praise the Lord! Our prayer is that he may be a real testimony to others. Please remember him in your prayers.

We all need your prayers. We want to do all that our Master asks us to do.

Yours in His glad service,
The Bernheim family
Emily Bernheim

• CHAPTER 15 •

May 27, 1937

My dear beloved in the Lord, one and all:

Praise Him for His great love and mercy that He has for us all. He surely does care for us, as He is very mindful of us even in this part of the world.

My family is going through a terrible test of malaria again. I am up, fighting my way out of bed. Emily is too far gone to write, but she still breathes, so there is still hope. I talk to her about the Lord and encourage her about the wonderful way God has of preparing His church for that great day, but we can't give up our task, which He has laid out for us. I trust in Him, the One Who rules heaven and earth and knows all things. I know you prayer warriors are busy praying for us and are surely mindful of us, for which we are more than happy.

What would we do if we all quit praying? Here in China we would have very little opportunity to do anything at all. There must be powerful prayer going up from you dear saints, or we would have gone to Jesus. I really think all of us would have gone, but that isn't what we're looking forward to.

I have the assurance the Lord is soon going to move mightily. Here are the reasons: the Chinese people listen eagerly. Second, white people are considered just people if we show them kindness and a sweet spirit. Third, white children can attract an immense crowd—we have crowds now whenever we go anywhere. Here in China if we want a crowd, we just walk toward town slowly, and stop when we have a sufficient crowd to witness to. We can all talk considerable Chinese. Fourth, the children are learning fast, and that is going to be a great advantage. Our washwoman often comes to the children with her Chinese song book (we bought two just like it), and we have a glorious time singing. Many of the tunes are just the same as we sing them in the USA.

I expect Mark to go out in the hills with me (the Lord willing) next time I go. I'm still all in, out, but not down, but you sweet saints have seen us through in prayer so far. Thank the Lord for you faithful prayer warriors and laborers in the gospel, for the gospel must be preached while it is day. It is for us to believe God and believe the Word that we are preaching.

Please press on in every way for the cause, for souls of the lost and dying people. Please pray more for us, as we are on your wire too. We know God is on the throne—He has never failed us in the fourteen years we have been serving Him, and He never changes—He is just the same today. We hope in God for Emily to be healed soon. The kiddies pray so earnestly for us that they might see us well. Praise Him; we have struck the vein of God's unlimited power. We couldn't live here without God's resurrecting power. We are so glad that we have the chance to suffer some with Him, then we shall also reign with Him. I'm so glad you dear one there are having some of the suffering too, that you too, may reign with Him. Let us be ready when the roll is called, and not found wanting.

Yours in the Masters service
Alfred Bernheim

• CHAPTER 16 •

Mr. Bernheim completes successful trip
Family undergoing persecution as foreigners

Kunming (Yunnanfu) S.W. China

June 12, 1937

Well, Hallelujah! Redeemed by the blood of the lamb! It is by His power that I am up again and able to write you a few lines. I do praise the Lord. It just seems as if every time the Lord has blessed us especially in a prayer meeting that the old devil jumps on someone. If I have counted rightly, I have been very ill for the sixth times now, but I'm still praising the Lord and as long as God is working, I plan to keep on saying Praise the Lord, even if the devil is mad. Of course, it's no wonder he is mad, for we are proclaiming the blood of Jesus and His power right on the devil's territory! We know that Jesus is our victory.

Several times we have been sick, the Lord has forewarned us of the sickness and promised us deliverance, but this time we were not warned. Although I know that we are not as good as Job was of old, yet I was greatly reminded of Job when Alfred and I were both taken sick this time. It seems as if I could almost hear old Satan's mocking words, "yes the other times you told them that they would be sick and that you would heal them, but just let me get hold of them without forewarning, when they are off their guard. They won't trust you then!" But again I shout "Hallelujah", for we did have the victory and trusted Him just the same. God is the same to deliver. It is by God's power that we are up.

Tomorrow, Lord willing, Alfred is planning on going on a special trip with the gospel message. He feels the Lord will strengthen him as he goes.

The children, too, have not been very well, but they trust in the Lord for full deliverance, and we know that we do not trust in vain.

Some people wish we were back in Spokane, where we wouldn't have to suffer so much. Well, I wish I were there, too, but just long enough to take those unbelievers by the back of the neck and give them a good shaking. Because I couldn't love and do for these people from afar off, as I can when I'm close by. And they couldn't hear very well or understand, either, unless I stay close beside them and talk plain Chinese language. So don't, anybody, wish me out of the will of the Lord, nor any of the rest of the Bernheim family. We all take pleasure in obeying the Lord, even the baby. She is a smiling young lady and before long will be preaching the gospel with words as well as smiles.

The Lord is blessing our street witnessing. Three girls have gone with me to Chinese meetings on two occasions. To assure us that God is working, one girl went all alone when I was not able to accompany her, so you can see that there is some seed growing in her heart. In the day of His appearing, we shall see what He has accomplished.

The prayer meetings are continuing to be blessed by the Lord. Each one seems to be better than the last. One young lady, who has been in China for about three years, said that the last one was the first real Pentecostal prayer meeting that she has been in since she left England.

As far as we can find out from here, no missionary is allowed to enter Tibet proper. As soon as a foreigner is discovered, the soldiers order him to leave in so many hours or be shot. A lady missionary that we know has entered several times by disguising herself as a man and traveling with a caravan, but as soon as she was found out, she had to leave and leave quickly. All the Tibetan work must be done on the border or in towns that once belonged to Tibet but have since been conquered by the Chinese.

The question of money is a real problem to anyone that wants to go to these places in the country. Silver money used to be used, but now the banks refused to give out anything but paper money, and the country people will not buy nor sell with the paper money, unless they have known you for years and even then it is impossible to get full value for the paper money. This is the problem that is facing missionaries that established stations in various places. Most of them buy enough food here to last six months or a year and ship it to their station in the country.

We have been trusting God for so long now and He has proved Himself so faithful that we have no fear of His not being able to supply our needs, even under those conditions. When God says, "Go", we are ready to go, whether we are equipped with all these things or not. We only wish He would say "go quickly", but He knows all things, so we feel that it is not our place to question Him as to why we, who are willing, have to wait.

We feel the same way about others in Spokane. When they have said "yes" to God, and are willing to go, He will show the time, just as He did to us in the past, and we are trusting Him for the future, that He will continue to be the head of all our comings and goings.

Yours for souls,
The Bernheim family

• CHAPTER 17 •

June 28, 1937

Dear loved ones in the homeland:

Praise the Lord, for He is worthy of praise. Let His name be magnified. Each time we look around and see the heathen darkness about us, we feel we have much to praise the Lord for. Although many have heard the gospel message, yet we see much darkness in this great land. We rejoice what we remember that the Lord has called as to preach salvation by grace, the gift of God. We have but one message for these dark hearts and that He is love. We know that love never fails, Praise His Holy Name.

Daily as we walk amongst these people, little children call us vile names. It takes a heart of love to love them when you know what they're saying. God supplies the needed grace. I have asked the Lord just what to say, as sometimes it seems as if I were just tongue-tied when they were mocking in such a way. What is most touching is that even the smallest babe can call you these vile names, and, of course, there is no re-proof or correction for the children of China. One day as I stepped out of my door I saw a large boy caring for two younger brothers. They seemed so tiny and innocent that I was surprised when the words, *bleating sheep* etc. fell from that dirty little baby's lips. God's love was greater than my feelings, so I stooped and took the little lambs by the hand and said, "I love you, and Jesus loves you, too". This touched the big brothers heart and he whispered to the babies not to say that anymore. Then as I continue talking of love to these little ones, tears sprang into his eyes. Words fail me. Tears in China. Yes, praise God, tears, from the heart. Now these two little babes no longer call me names, but rather they say, "Oh, teacher please, we want some bread". So bread they must have if there is any to give them. They eat it with a-relish, as one can see they are very poor. It is for these that Christ died.

Mr. Bernheim had a blessed time in the country giving forth the message of God's love, handing out gospels, and witnessing in gambling tea shops, etc. The devil is hard on our trail, so after this blessed time of witnessing for the Lord, Mr. Bernheim accidentally drank some very bad water, and became very ill. His body began to bloat, but God was mighty and answered prayer. We must rejoice over such a wonderful Savior. Alfred says that he is going out preaching just as long as he has breath, by God's grace and power. God's will must be worked out in our lives. God does give us joy and peace, in knowing that we are doing his will.

The angel of death is still hovering over Yunnanfu. Three have died in the compound from which we moved. Now it has come into the house we are living in, only in the other half. Praise God for the dividing line. One is dead now and another is dying in the rooms in the other half of our house. And there are others dying all around us. Oh how we need your prayers that we might be under God's protection. We want to live that we might witness for our Lord, and we need prayer. By God's grace, we shall be delivered.

The robbers have not yet given up trying to enter our house. God has again awakened Alfred that he might stop them before they

Becky Croasmun

entered our rooms. So we continue to praise Him for He never slumbers or sleeps.

When this letter reaches you, it will have been almost a year since we left Spokane. What a short year it has been! A time of testing through sickness such as we had never before experienced, yet a time when joy and glory from above have not ceased flow. We know that God is working although we do not yet see the full results of our labors. That is not for us to see, nor is it for us to question, it is but ours to follow His command.

We do wish to thank you all for your support to us in funds and prayers. May God reward you every one. You are the rope holders of this great work for the master. And, verily, God will see that you hold not in vain. God bless you all.

Yours for souls,
The Bernheim family

(Printed below is a letter from Esther Bernheim, written to the Sunday school class she belonged to before she sailed for China. The members of the class have named themselves *Jesus Helpers* and we are printing this letter in order that other *Jesus Helpers,* big and little, may have a chance to read it.)

Dear Jesus Helpers,

How are you all? We are all quite fine.

I guess you children would like to know how the town looks. All the houses are made of mud. I don't know if you children know how the streets look or not. They look very queer. They are made of rocks. They have bricks, but not like our American bricks. They are made of mud. We have mud hens, too, over here by the pond. The pond is just some very bad smelling water. The mosquitoes carry typhoid. The Chinese have a five cent copper about as big as an American dollar.

I am glad God let me come to China. Of course, it is not as nice as it is in America, but there are lots of things to do for Jesus, as the people here worship idols instead of God. So I am learning Chinese as fast as I can so that I can tell them more and more about Jesus. I am saving up all my coppers so we can buy an organ, as I like to play and the Chinese like music. All of us sing Chinese songs, but an organ will help us in many ways. But mamma says it takes 20 coppers to make three pennies, but I am praying that the Lord will help me get an organ as we could learn the tunes better if we had one. I wish you would pray, too, so I get one soon.

Well, I guess I better close for now. Goodbye.

Esther Bernheim

• CHAPTER 18 •

Kunming, Yunnan Province

July 21, 1937

Dear loved ones in America:

I have been unusually busy, as Alfred has gone to the country and expects to be gone some time. Being alone, I have more responsibilities than when he is home. Somehow I always depend on Alfred, or rather I depend on the Lord's awakening Alfred in case of robbers (which He always did), but now I must depend on His awakening me, and on the whole, I feel I must be quite alert. I am trying to so walk that the Lord will be able to speak to me, if I should be needed night or day.

I caught enough rain to fill a bathtub yesterday morning when it was raining, so we are still on dry ground. The Lord is causing much surplus water to vanish and my wash woman joins me in saying, *Somma Yasu*, or *Praise Jesus*, as she has been worrying for fear we should be drowned out.

In the last letter I told you about having a casket in the other half of the house. Well, it is buried now. The day the woman died, the casket was ordered, the parlor cleared, and a casket prepared for the body and placed in the parlor. Much flimsy silk was used for the lining of the casket and for decorations. The casket was placed behind white drapes and a picture of the woman was hung up over a little table that held paper flowers and idols. Red silk banners were made for the occasion. Four nights later, twelve red robed priests chanted and drummed before the casket for about three hours. I did not see them, but I heard it all through the walls.

We waited and waited, expecting the rest of the funeral. We heard that sometimes the bodies are kept for months. Finally one day much cooking was done and guests came to eat. In the evening the priests in the bright red robes once again made music and chanted. The head priest was crowned to represent Buddha. Candles and incense were burning during all the ceremony. They burned paper money because the soul did not take enough along when it died. The ones in mourning did not seem a bit sorry, but seemed to enjoy the entertainment that the priest was offering them. About 11:30 p.m. the priest took off the robes that they wore and ate all the food that had been offered to the idols. The next day all the banners and paper images and several floats were paraded to the cemetery. The casket was covered with red silk embroidered with dragons and cranes. There was more feasting after they came back from the cemetery.

It made our hearts ache because they had not believed on Jesus. We had witnessed to them so we feel that our hands are clear,

I must not forget to ask you all to help us pray for the organ that Esther mentioned in her letter. For about $30 American money one can buy quite a serviceable one. Of course they are Chinese make, they have good tones and I have been told that they last quite well. We try to help the copper fund as much as possible, but I know that saving coppers is a long job for kiddies, so won't you please pray that the Lord will give Esther a special offering for her organ?

Becky Croasmun

One thing we are grateful for is that summer has brought us some native fruit. Naturally I am regretting that I have no jars or canning equipment, but still I am glad we can eat it while it is in season. Oh we have so many things to be thankful for! Our joys may be untold, but hallelujah for what we feel!

Do not forget us in prayer. There is war at the capital, and the anti-foreign spirit is affecting Yunnan. Some people don't know the difference between Americans and Japanese; all they know is that you are not Chinese, and—woe is you!

Yours, standing in the breach,
The Bernheim family

• CHAPTER 19 •

Brother Bernheim tells of his experiences in recent trip

P'ing An Kai, No 7
Kunming (Yunnanfu)
Yunnan Province, S.W. China

August 9, 1937

Dear loved ones in the homeland,

Greetings to you all in the name of our dear Savior. He who trod the way before us. Praise and honor and glory be to His Holy name.

I believe you will be interested in hearing about my experiences in a recent country trip. Brother Jones of England was taking the same journey, so we traveled together. Neither of us had ever experienced such a hard dangerous journey in China. The Lord gave us the scriptures found in John 14:12-14 and Matthew 18:19, 20 as we started our journey, so that we were filled with overflowing with His Spirit and we knew we had nothing to fear. Little did anyone realize what would take place in the near future.

The first night we spent among some Pentecostal people. Arrangements were immediately made for a meeting. The meeting place had no other floor than just the bare ground. But God was there with mighty power. It happened to be market day. Some people walked as far as 50 Chinese miles to attend the meeting and they were not disappointed, because God met them there. Such fiery singing and praises such as ascended unto God that night are rarely found, and the angels in heaven joined in with the music, for a number of souls surrendered to God that night. The house was packed and the streets were crowded as they drank in the words of eternal life.

Most of the journey was by horses and mules. I was forced to walk many times when my horse, that was young and frisky, ran away until I caught up with him again. There were no stirrups, bits, bridle, leading rein or saddle. These pack horses carry a *jotzda*, which is a wooden foundation having two sockets into which fits a wooden frame. A strap passes around the back legs and around the shoulders of the horse preventing the frame going backwards or forward. When loads are being carried, they are tied to this frame. This frame rises to a narrow surface at the top, and it was on the top of this that we were to perch! That is a painful experience, and even when the horse is steady and the road smooth. But we had neither. My horse was weak in the knees and often stumbled head first giving me many a tumble. Once the horse rolled on top of me, another time I was right under the horse and was very thankful that I was able to get out before he moved his feet.

The nights were spent in various inns. We were nearly eaten up with flies, fleas and mosquitoes. The surface of the food chopping blocks would be just black with flies; just before the cook at the inn would chop up fresh food, he would wave his hand at the flies and then go ahead with his chopping! The horseman were heavy drinkers of whiskey and spent many hours of the night screaming and shouting, making it impossible to sleep. One needs the strength received from the prayers of others in order to keep sweet and to witness under such circumstances. One night after the drinking was all over, the landlord placed the whiskey urn in our room for safekeeping. We were drinking of the Living Water from the fountain that never runs dry, so we did not find any temptation in the earthen urn.

We climbed many rocky mountains reaching a high altitude and came into what seemed a different land. There were blue rocks, green grass and ferns. Almost everything was different from the lower country, the scenery and the weather especially. It is very hot and wet all summer and very cold in the winter.

This was very dangerous robber country where the robbers murder their victims first and plunder afterwards. Fearing the robbers, the horsemen travel in large bands. We joined ourselves to an unusually large one containing over 2000 horses. We could see horses on the trail ahead of us and behind us five or six abreast. I want to break into the narrative here to say that when the Lord first gave me my call to China, He showed me just such a caravan of horses as this traveling through country like this. As we went on our way, I realized that this was just what God had shown me. Perhaps some of you will remember that that was the time when I prayed through; praying until I felt I could stand for God, even though my arms and legs should be cut off. I have testified to this many times.

After we joined this party, early in the day we met a group of travelers who told us that the robbers were active, especially one band over 60 strong. Many of the horsemen carried pistols, rifles and knives. We were told that 1000 farmers have banded together to go out after the robbers. Later when we passed a village, we were told that the robbers had ambushed the farmers, shot and killed two of them and escaped. It was only too true.

Arriving at the midday of resting place, which was a bunch of mud and straw hovels, we were very fortunate to be able to obtain a little refreshment (two poached eggs apiece and water) boiled in a greasy pot) to make tea. This was a treat considering all the things that were confronting us.

Then the whole caravan started off. The road was cut out of a very steep mountain, which on the inner side was almost straight up and on the outer side was almost straight down. Most pack animals are mules and act accordingly. Here on this narrow road, the mules became crowded and a mad scramble and fight ensued. With loads standing out on both sides, each mule fought to force his way forward. Others, resenting the pressure, flashed their iron shod heels in rapid motion. Brother Jones was in the middle of the fight with his mule and was in danger of being crushed or kicked to death. I was on the outer edge. The other horses were being pushed over the edge and my mule already had his hind legs over that dangerous precipice. The frantic, foolish horsemen were helplessly screaming and shouting, and could do nothing. The Lord undertook just as I was ready to jump off my mule and He miraculously put my mule back on the road. And as they got straightened out, Brother Jones was put into a place of comparative safety. The horsemen had realized that so many mules constituted a serious danger, but they were all frightened over the murder they had heard about that morning and were anxious to leave immediately after lunch, as they thought it was either that or be murdered and robbed.

The next day the rain poured down and with it came bloodshed and murder. When we started out soldiers searched everyone for silver, which is now worth more than the face value because the government has called it in and replaced it with paper money. Crooked horseman transport and sell the silver, which necessitates soldiers searching every party of horsemen. The soldiers confiscate all the silver they found.

Some time previous to this, three honest horsemen in our company had reported four dishonest ones to the officers for trading opium and silver, and these dishonest men were punished. They were now free and traveling with us. At the midday resting place, these four men came up to the three who had reported them and shot them dead. They had their revenge. Not one amongst all those who were eyewitnesses dared to give evidence, because they were afraid for their own lives.

The rain continued to pour down, and the road was a bog. We were shivering in cold, wet clothes. Brother Jones had on a light cape designed for walking, and that cape was the cause of a rather amusing incident. He had a man hold his mule while he mounted from a high bank. When he straddled the high jotzda, the tight cape tied his hands to his side. Before he could get his hands loose, the man gave the mule a whack, and with a yell started the mule up the steep bank. Brother Jones was absolutely helpless and couldn't hang on, so he just tipped backwards ever so gently, turning a somersault over the mule's tail and landing on his head (with his big coolie hat still on) deeply embedded in the

71

soft mud. He looked just like a beautiful flower planted upside down! The crowd roared and so did he. This spill made the blood circulate afresh, driving away the shivers so that he glowed all over with warmth.

I had had a rain cape and leggings, but they were lost in the turmoil, so my legs and feet were wet all the time. The jotdza was so painful, the roads were so difficult; we were so wet and so blistered and crippled, that we were very thankful to God when we arrived at the evening rest place.

Since my animal was short legged, it was usually at the end of the caravan as it seemed unable to keep up with the others, but on this afternoon I had managed to keep in the center of the caravan. Some, who had loitered along the road, arrived in groups much later than the main caravan. One of the groups had been attacked by robbers, one man seriously wounded in the stomach and shoulder, another shot through the wrist, etc.

Soon the Chinese had settled down to their opium smoking and gambling in the room just below our sleeping quarters. The opium fumes build our lungs all during the night. Brother Jones speaks Chinese quite freely, and he felt led to go downstairs and give them all a clear witness about the Lord. I stayed up above on my knees, praying for Brother Jones and the men he was talking to, and from below they were able to hear me as a Spirit of God bubbled over in me. Glory to His name! God's Word went forth and His Spirit also, and we believe God used both to His honor and glory.

At last we reached Loping. It is walled on three sides by jagged mountains, like dragon's teeth, sharp stones of all sizes piled up one behind the other, thousands and thousands of them. They seem to tear up the clouds and fling the water to the ground in a deluge. The heavens get angry at a moment's notice. So much rain makes even midsummer boiling hot at one moment and bitterly cold at the next. Between rains, the sun shines on the drenched air and steams one's strength away.

When we felt that our work and witnessing for the Lord was finished in Loping for the present time, we started toward Yunnanfu and home.

On the first day's journey we accompanied Mr. Huu, the bank investigator of the silver problem, and Captain Chang, appointed to suppress the opium traffic. Captain Chang was really a very fine man and was deeply impressed, and seemed to love me very much. We coveted him for the Lord. With him was an escort of soldiers, and two prisoners, suspected of murder. Captain Chang was very kindhearted. He raved and swore at his men because the prisoners had not been fed, and all along the way, he tried to see that there was food for them. (Of course, in America, that would not be so unusual, but compared to the rest of the men we had been in contact with, he was a very fine man, indeed, and he drank in the gospel message like a child. He was very different from the man he was to take the prisoners to.)

My horse for the return journey was even friskier than the first one. One time he unexpectedly sent me spinning to the ground, which was very hard and dry as it was just before the rain in that particular locality, and I fell flat on my face, crushing my nose.

The blood streamed freely, but I was still rejoicing in the Lord. Later as we journeyed, we came to a huge hole by the side of the road, where the animals must go very close beside it and from our dangerous perch on the jotdza, we had a very good chance to look into the apparently bottomless pit. God again had his hand outstretched in protection, because, had the horses reared in any way, or the earth given away beneath us, we could only to easily have fallen to our death with no chance of a rescue. It is claimed that that whole has no bottom.

Soon we were confronted by a band of men with cocked revolvers. The Captain and his troops had now left us, and just three soldiers remained to guard the prisoners. The leader of this band pointed to one prisoner and said "He is an honest man". This proved to be true, and he was later untied when the road police gave evidence to that effect, but the prisoners still had to appear before the magistrate that night.

The police told us that robbers were active. Fifty-two soldiers had been appointed to guard that road, but the robbers had shot a goodly number and the rest refused to stay. Later we again met Captain Chang, who was guarding that road. He was as fearless as he was kind, and with his soldiers he scoured the woods on each side of the path, galloping up every vantage point to view the road, and searching and questioning every traveler.

After lunch the weather became stifling. A number of thunderstorms broke in the hills around, but missed us. Then we came to a vast plain. Piled high above the banks of black clouds that were stretched across the plain from horizon to horizon was a long black line. Then the lightning began to viciously stab and shoot from both ends, progressing toward the center, and tearing up the clouds with terrific force. They began to empty out at a deluge of water. Soon the clouds were all broken up and the water was falling like a sheet ahead of us. The air around us chilled and a fierce wind arose. The horses began to whinny and grow restless. In another fifteen minutes the storm struck us with such a blast of fury that it almost carried horses, loads and men into the ditch.

As we had not expected rain, our rain clothes were locked away. In a few seconds we were drenched to the skin by the icy rain and our clothes were dragging off of us with the weight of the water. The horses wheeled and crouched low, shivering with cold and fear. The thunder was like a battery of cannons roaring in our ears. The lightning was incessant and blinding. The hailstones were like marbles. A bitterly cold blast of wind drove the huge raindrops almost horizontal.

We stood for a while by the horses, while the road changed into a bog. We soon began to shiver and shake; we could not control our limbs, and we were shaking so violently that we were almost unable to stand. We realized that to stand still would be to die of cold, so we forged forward through the driving blast with the main swishing around our feet, staggering through the deep mud and the torrents that poured across the road.

Once before in a heavy storm Brother Jones and I sang duets which had deeply impressed the captain, but now the fierceness of the blast and the intense cold made us pant and gasp through clenched teeth as we fought our way along hour after hour. Words could never describe the misery of that afternoon. The storm was so fierce that that the horse carrying our load lost it in the mud and ran away frantically and it was only after much trouble that the horsemen caught the horse and reloaded the load. The calves of my legs were bleeding from rubbing on the jotzda and the mud and water in my shoes made my feet bleed and pain; in fact, the tip of my big toe was completely worn off. But we had no choice: we must either walk or die in the cold.

Evening brought the edge of the storm and the stopping place for the night which was just an empty house with no fire, food or hot water. While we were waiting for our horses and goods, we once more began to shiver. Finally a Chinese man gave us some hot water to drink and some more to wash in. When the horses arrived, we found that most of our clean clothes were wet. Fortunately, I had two dry shirts, so I was able to loan Brother Jones one. A brisk rub down and dry clothes certainly felt good.

Then the captain graciously invited us to supper. Beside a good fire, we were once more bubbling over with the joy of the Lord and ready to give witness to the power of God unto salvation.

After supper we visited the Chief Magistrate, a man of great power and greatly feared. The most interesting thing in his room was the opium lounge. It seemed odd that the Captain was coming to give his report on the suppression of opium smugglers, and yet the Mandarin, himself, was a heavy smoker with a luxurious lounge. There were two long crimson bolster pillows and two crimson mattresses with a fancy opium lamp between them and big opium a pipe studded with mother of pearl.

Soon the Magistrate came in, very tall and impressive, dressed in a beautiful brown gown. After introducing us, the Captain gave his report, explaining that the prisoners were proved innocent. The Mandarin stuttered with anger as he exclaimed, "You should take no chances! You should kill them!" We realized that, as the Captain had informed us previously, this was a cruel and a hard man. He commanded the prisoners to be brought in, looked them over, and ordered them away. What happened to them we don't know, but we hope that they were released?

I was sitting on a high stool, with my eyes closed, from time to time tipping forward from sheer exhaustion, and in the dimly lighted room, a Brother Jones said that I looked like a dozing chicken on a roost. The Mandarin noticed my weariness and invited me to rest on the opium lounge, which after a little persuasion I did, and at once was sound asleep; as I had had little or no rest for many nights before.

About an hour later, we were called to supper, the second that night, and how good it was! The Mandarin plied us with many questions about our religion, and, pointing to portraits of three of China's greatest men, he said, "They believed in Jesus Christ". We answered his question as God led us to, with no stiffness or formality. We had become good friends, brought together by the fierce storm. Although we were weary and longed for bed, we expected that they would detain us till, perhaps, two a.m., but happily they released us shortly after ten p.m. Our beds and blankets were wet, making the night quite miserable, but God kept us from chilling.

We met with much antagonism and prejudice in various places, and felt more of an anti-foreign spirit than ever before. They often try to provoke a quarrel with us by flinging our goods about and cursing us as dogs of foreign devils, using dreadful terms. Although it is Japan that is waging war on China, and yet to the average inland Chinese man or woman, Japanese and other foreigners are all alike. God help us to stand as good soldiers of Jesus Christ.

The last inn we stopped at was very different from most of them. The two landladies were extremely kind and helped us all they could. The inn was so small that men, horses, cows, cats, pigs, ducks, dogs, mosquitoes, flies and fleas all slept together in one small place.

For many days our mouths had been skinned raw through trying to eat the Chinese dishes made with red pepper, as this is the red pepper season. The Chinese seem immune to it, but we could no longer eat these peppery dishes and the pain in our mouths prevented us from sleeping. At 11:30 p.m. the landlady came downstairs to prepare breakfast. The bright moonlight must have made her think that day was breaking. Her chopping kindling awakened the horsemen who awakened the rest, saying that day was breaking. We had wanted to get home the next day, but it seemed rather hopeless to attempt it, but now we wondered if, perhaps, the Lord wasn't making it possible by arousing everyone at that time. As we couldn't sleep anyway, we were very glad to arise, singing, and whistling, to greet the dawn at 11:30 p.m. as we washed, packed and prepared to travel. The horsemen hastily watered and fed the horses. By that time breakfast was ready. We had decided to turn our watches the two hours ahead, so now when the horsemen ask us the time we said "Our watches say 3:30, but they are not reliable". This is true, as foreign watches do not keep good time in China. It must have been about 1:30 at the time, but the horsemen were positive that our watches were slow! We ate a hasty meal while the lightning flashed, the thunder rolled, and the rain empty down. They waited and waited for the dawn, and some of them blamed the rain for its non-appearance. Eventually we started out in the dark. We staggered through lakes and ponds, it seemed, and it took all our energy to cling to the horses. We had traveled a long way before dawn came.

What a dreadful day that was, in some ways. We were sore and worn and weary, and yet we were happy. Happy, first, because we had been in the Master's service, second, because we hoped to be home to cleanliness and more comfort that night, and third, because God had promised to keep us and He had fulfilled His promise. Blessed be the Name of the Lord. He is always faithful. Oh, for faith to trust Him more!

We arrived home about 8:00 p.m. that night, where our families were waiting for us. And together, we rejoiced in the knowledge of God's care while we were absent one from the other.

Yours in the Master's service till He comes,
Alfred Max Bernheim

Dear Office Staff and Readers,

I, indeed, do thank God for being with us at home while Alfred was away. God kept us well and guarded us with His angels. An intruder tried to enter the house while we were alone, but was unsuccessful. He merely broke through on to a tin sheet that gives us shelter from the rain and God used that in keeping us in safety. We rejoice in Him at all times.

Alfred kept perfectly well on the trip, but has been very ill since he came home, with malaria and cold. But God has graciously touched him, so that he is up again.

We are praising the Lord for the rainy season, as it will mean rice for the Chinese, and they have had so little and such poor rice in the last few years. At the same time it is a trial, because our downstairs is so stuffy and the rain comes through upstairs making our bedding wet. But it is not for us to murmur and complain, but to praise and follow on. Pray with us that if He feels us worthy of a better home, we might get one.

David has been very ill, but also was healed by the Lord. We praise Him for victory through the blood.

God bless you all for the interest you are taking in this work in offerings and prayers. Without prayer we could not stand. We shall all be remembered when God opens the account books in that great day.

Yours for the Master,
Emily Bernheim

● CHAPTER 20 ●

BERNHEIMS IN THE WAR ZONE

Dear loved ones at home:

"When ye see these things begin to come to pass… lift up your heads and rejoice, for your redemption draweth nigh" (Luke 21:28). We find ourselves in that place at the present time; "wars and rumors of wars" so close to our door that we know not what a day shall bring forth. Yet we praise God for the victory that we possess in Christ Jesus, our Lord and Savior.

War conditions are very distressing, indeed. There is bombing not far from here, and this town also has been threatened. Our hope is in God, for He knows what lies before us, and we would not shrink from His will. We can but stand in the gap and point souls to Jesus, beseeching them to believe on Him and to call upon Him in prayer, for all help cometh from God. That is our message to the people in these days, as we meet them and see that they are distressed over the condition that sweeps the land. So we covet your prayers more earnestly that ever before that these few words may indeed be remembered and heeded.

The typhoon on the coast has also caused great distress, tossing two large ships from the waters on dry land. One ship carrying mail was sunk in that disaster, and we think that is why some of our letters have not arrived.

For ourselves, we can live but one day at a time. Rumors of evacuation are becoming quite serious. We know that God will care for us and not permit anything to befall us that is not His will. We are here only because we obeyed His command, not counting ourselves or anything of ours dear, for all is His, and we, ourselves, belong to Him.

It seems advisable from now on to send mail to us via Europe, as then it does not go through Japanese or Chinese hands until two days' journey from us.

> P'ing An Kai, No 7
> Kunming (Yunnanfu)
> Yunnan Province
> S.W. China (via Europe)

Thank you all for your prayers and offering that you have sent that the work of God might go forth. God bless you all is our prayer.

Yours, witnessing for the Master,
The Bernheim Family

• CHAPTER 21 •

September 22, 1937

Dear loved ones in the homeland:

"I love the Lord, because He had heard my voice and my supplication. Because He has inclined His ear unto me, therefore will I call upon Him as long as I shall live" (Psalms 116:1-2).

Just one year has passed since we arrived in Yunnanfu. What a glorious year it has been! A year in which we have learned to love and trust the Lord for greater things and in greater measure than ever before.

The letters that we have written from time to time speak of sicknesses that we have suffered, but more of the power of God that has delivered us from the jaws of death. Hallelujah to His precious Name! We have proven that nothing is too hard for the Master.

We are earnestly waiting on the Lord at this time to find where He would have us go. We are surrounded by war and by robbers, and no one knows what will overtake the country next, so we are praying earnestly to know the will of God. We feel a great responsibility, not only for our own lives, but also for those of our six children, as should we make a wrong move, our lives might be cut off instantly. Not that we are afraid to die! No, that is not it, for when we are cut off from this life, real life in the presence of God begins. But when we think of the work that is to be done for the Master, we feel it more needful to live and to witness in the heat or in storm, that souls may see Jesus our Savior and have life also.

About a month ago, we felt led of God to pack so now we are ready for some move. We have not had any definite orders from God but what this move shall be, so we are waiting till He reveals His perfect will. The Lord has given us many dreams, preparing us for the move that we will make soon. We believe in His time, He will make known what is the proper way to go.

We thank the Lord for yielded lives. Our prayer is "Let us to yield more and more to Thee." At this time of writing, we are all well. Praise the Lord for victory on that point. How we covet your prayers at this time. We are helpless in these days on this field unless we have prayer.

"God bless you all" is our prayer.

Yours, at the battle front, for Jesus,
The Bernheim family.

• CHAPTER 22 •

Hokow
Yunnan Province
S.W. China

November 25, 1937

Dear Saints in the homeland,

"There is therefore now no condemnation to them which are in Christ Jesus, who walk not after the flesh, but after the Spirit". Following the leading of the Spirit, we are now in Hokow, a place where much witnessing for the Master is needed, and where we can reach many people that come from various places.

It was only after much prayer and waiting upon the Lord that we came here. The Lord gave us an open door immediately, but Satan did his best to close it. The battle lasted about three weeks, but God undertook, the victory was won, and the open door could not be closed.

Read Romans 8:18, 35 through 39, knowing that these things have been a reality to us. We rejoice in the Lord, because He is greater than all.

Now that we are pioneers in this new field, we need your prayers more than ever before. Times and seasons prevent us from writing much, but we trust that God will reveal all that we cannot write to you, as He has in the past.

Becky Croasmun

In the natural, this field is shunned by all missionaries. The climate is unfavorable and deadly; living prices are double to what they were, but we trust in our God who is greater than all. Had we been following the natural man, we would not be here, but the need, shown to us by God, of this people for whom Christ died prompted us to lay all at His feet, that we might come and give to this people a witness and a chance to receive eternal life. It would have been healthier some other place, but it seems as if the people who live in unhealthy places need the gospel, too, before they die.

Brother Jones and his family are planning on going to England for a short time, and then, Lord willing come to Spokane and see all you dear ones. They are worthy of Philadelphian fellowship, for they count not their own lives dear, but look to the Lord for all things. So should they arrive in Spokane about spring, they come at our invitation. They are not connected with any church and have very little support, but trust God for all their needs. We have certainly learned to love them, and already we look for the time when they shall return to the field.

Brother and Sister Jones gave us their new organ, to be paid for as the Lord provides, so we are rejoicing over that. Everyone in town knows we have an organ.

We thank the Lord for all the news that we received through your letters and the Church Message, and we also thank you all for your offerings and support and your prayers, for, if we did not have them, we could not stand. We have all been undergoing a great physical suffering this last month, and the spiritual burden and groaning also have taken much strength and have given us sleepless nights. But we continue to look to Jesus, the Author and Finisher of our faith; our strength, yea; He is our all in all. The peace and victory we feel is greater than the suffering we have endured.

Yours for the Master,
The Bernheim family

• CHAPTER 23 •

HoKow, Yunnan Province, S.W. China

December 17, 1937

Dear Loved Ones in the Homeland:

"Bless the Lord, O my soul, and all that is within me, bless His holy Name. Bless the Lord, O my soul and forget not all His benefits" Psalms 103:1.

Here in HoKow we find ourselves praising the Lord for many things. We praise Him for the lessons we have learned in the past, and we are so glad that His grace and strength is sufficient day by day.

While we were coming, the Lord told us that what we were going through then was to make a stronger for the things that were ahead of us. Now as we look back, the things that are past seem like nothing, merely a stepping stone. So we know that where we are now and the tests that befall us day by day are just stepping stone to some greater work that the Lord will do later. As we stand pointing souls to Christ, we pray that the seed sown may fall on good ground and accomplish the Father's will.

Here in Hokow we not only reach the local people, but also tribes' people that come here to trade. We give portions of God's Word and message of love to them, and God alone knows the end of it all, as they carry the message back to their own villages. Some of every tribe and nation will be there when we all gather round the throne, Hallelujah! Does that not make your heart rejoice?

We need your prayers much. Brother Bernheim has been suffering daily from malaria since we have been here. Words cannot describe his suffering and it is only the power of God that keeps him alive. Alfred is much run down, as this fever surely takes all one's strength. He has no appetite. One day I prepared him a chicken, hoping he would be able to eat it, but he could only look at it. But we know that God is true to His promise that our strength is as our day. Through all of this, Alfred is pressing on, standing firm in the faith by the power of God, and taking Him for His all in all. He feels that God is preparing him for something hard ahead, and by God's grace, he wants to follow all the way.

Alfred joins heartily in praise to God that the rest of the family are well at present. The baby was very sick after we left Kunming, but God has raised her up and she is feeling fine now. She is walking all around, scattering sunshine as she goes. Esther and David have almost received the infilling of the Holy Spirit since we came here and Mark and Ruthie have been a great blessing.

We pray that you will continue to hold us up to the Throne of Grace, that we might be yielded vessels for the Master's use.

Yours for Soul till Jesus comes,
The Bernheim Family

• CHAPTER 24 •

HoKow, Yunnan Province
S.W. China

January 05, 1938

Dear Loved Ones in the Homeland:

Again we greet you from far away China. We rejoice day by day as we see that Jesus is just the same yesterday, today and forever. Some people may say that the day of miracles is past, but had you been in Hokow during the last few weeks, you would not be counted among those unbelievers. We wrote that Brother Bernheim was suffering terribly with malaria. Day by day he continued to get worse. He would have chills, and then fever for hours at a time, suffering indescribable agony until the sweat would roll from his body by the sheets. But he would soon be weak and exhausted, and then the same thing would happen over again.

Somehow I felt that it was God's will to heal him, yet he kept getting worse and worse. I put him on the altar, not just once, but every day, till at last, when I could see him suffer no longer, I cried, "Oh Lord, if you don't see fit to heal him, take him home! Anything to relieve him from this terrible suffering. Lord, thy will be done".

His legs were cold and numb almost to his hips, his head was cold and the rattle of death was it his throat. He had praised the Lord until his voice was gone and he could do so no longer, "Oh, Jesus, let me go". He moaned.

I never saw or heard anyone closer to death than he was, when at last God, in His mighty power, sent the victory, rebuked death, and set him free. Hallelujah! So now you may join us in praise to God for His power made manifest.

It was on Christmas night that Alfred had that last attack of malaria, and the fever left and has not returned, so it was a glad day after all.

Brother Bernheim is still very weak from all that he suffered, but he is gaining strength and is able to sit up in an easy chair. His heart still seems week and pounds hard, and his feet and legs are swollen, so please continue to hold him up in prayer.

When Jesus was on earth, it was said, "And He must needs go through Samaria" where, although He was hungry and thirsty He stopped to witness to the Samaritans before continuing His journey. So, it seems to us that we have stopped here where no one else was willing to come that this people should have the gospel witness before the coming of the Lord. Although we have suffered much to bring the gospel here, yet we feel we have done our duty to coming to them.

Lois and Mark have also been sick, but God has touched them. We are so glad we can trust God in China just as we did in the homeland: He never changes but grows more precious every day. We feel that we are the wiser for every experience that God has sent our way.

• CHAPTER 25 •

January 21, 1938

We wish to thank you all for your love and prayers and offerings. Words cannot express our appreciation to God and you dear ones for standing by so faithfully as we endeavor to point souls to Him.

God has answered prayer for Brother Bernheim's health, so that he is able to walk around now and has a good appetite. To good for this country, as we cannot get the things he would like to eat. But he is thankful for a good missionary stomach that is able to digest the food that we can obtain. We find many things to be thankful for.

We feel that the Lord is calling us to work farther in the interior, and we are making preparations to start. We covet your continued prayers as we live only to serve Him and to follow His commands.

Conditions at present handicap us from writing much, but we know that we are in God's protecting care and He will not permit anything that we are not able to bear

Cheerfully in His Service
The Bernheim Family

Interesting notes on everyday life in the interior of China, from a personal letter from the Bernheim's: "We sleep on boards with some blankets. We sleep on more or less blankets as the winter permits. If it is warm, we put them under us and if it turns colder, we pull them out to cover up with. The wood worms saw in the wood day and night, playing us a tune all the time. My bed is pretty well sawed up. And spiders! The spiders are so big they cluck like a rooster. Just yesterday one was hiding in the roof beams that clucked very loud just like a rooster calling his hens. We saw one that measured eight inches of across."

Bernheims, 1936 before China

On Our Way to China, August, 1936

Ma Ka, China

Song Ling, China
X is Emily

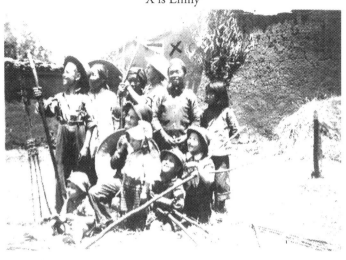

Kids on neighbors water buffalo

Kunming with kids and neighbors

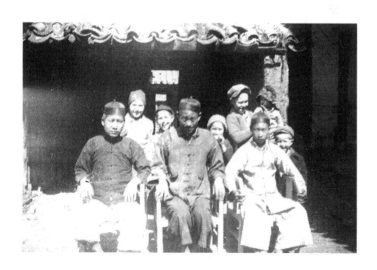

Market Place

Grave Site

L to R John, Esther, Lois, Ruth, Mark

The Phillips House
Kowloon, China

Rev. Charles and Lydia Hollandsworth

Bernheim Boy Is Proud Possessor of Accordion

Jerry Owen, revivalist at the Apostolic tabernacle, recently presented this accordion to Mark Bernheim, 15-year-old son of the Rev. and Mrs. A. M. Bernheim, missionaries, who were killed last year in China. His brother and three sisters looking on, from left to right, are Esther, Lois, John and Ruth. The children are now making their home with their aunt and uncle, the Rev. and Mrs. C. R. Hollandsworth, E1108 Eleventh.

Philip Hanson Jones

L to R Lois, John, Ruth, Esther, Mark (1967)

• CHAPTER 26 •

Hokow Yunnan Province, S.W. China

Dear Loved Ones:

Greetings to you all from China, God bless you all.

We are so glad that we can still report victory, victory through the blood of the Lamb that was slain. Day by day we see victory as we go among these people as messengers of the Life that is theirs through the power of God. We see signs of an awakening among the children and among their parents when they nod their heads to us or ask us to come and join them as they are seated on their stools. Praise the Lord! These words may not seem so very much to you, but if you had been here, had suffered the powers of darkness and felt the bondage that sin can bring, then you too, would shout *Victory!* It is better felt than told.

Best of all, we have the promise of God that His Word shall not return unto Him void, and many people can now read the Words of Life in the gospels that have been given them. So when we are gathered around the throne, I'm sure that some from HoKow and the tribes around will also be among the number. From every tribe and nation there will be some representatives.

Since last writing, Brother Bernheim has again been very ill, with a sudden very serious attack of the malaria. But God in His mighty power brought the victory. So we again give thanks unto the Lord

Becky Croasmun

Oh, how we covert your prayers in these days! Pray for these souls to whom we have given the gospel that God's light may shine brightly into their hearts. Pray for us that God will give us the strength and power that we need to stand against the evil powers that surround us. Pray for the children, the Chinese children, and our own children, too. The children are doing their part in helping to scatter the gospel, as with joy, they give out the little gospel booklets and tell the Chinese that Jesus has eternal life for them. The children also take great comfort in saying, "Well, when we get to Heaven, then we'll know how much good was done. So we'll just keep on doing it for Jesus". Many people might have felt discouraged if they had been in China for over a year and yet had not seen many visible results, but if it is not for us to see the increase, we know that God sees, and that is enough. It makes our hearts rejoice when we know that children, too, think about these things. So do not forget them in your prayers.

We do thank you all for your love and prayers and the offerings that make it possible for God's work to go on. Prices are just about three times what they used to be. Traveling expenses also have increased. But we must go where He bids us sow the seed at God's command.

We hear very little news about the war. This province, we are told is only a few hours by air from the captured places. Some missionaries have gone to Hong Kong or to America to wait until everything is over. Our trust is in the Lord; He can keep us.

Our house is made of mud brick with two floors. The downstairs is partitioned off into two small rooms and a hall, and the upstairs is all one room. We live upstairs as the downstairs is too wet and moldy. Even upstairs our betting, shoes and clothing turn green with mold. The weather is very changeable; one day may be blistering hot, the next cold or rainy. One never knows what to expect. The roof of our house is high and made of tile. Most houses in China have the reputation of having a leaky roof and ours is no exception. Often the rain comes down on the beds but we praise the Lord just the same.

How did we happen to come here to Hokow? First, we heard that it was a vast, untouched field. Second, almost every time that we mentioned to anyone that we might go into the country, that person would tell us about this vast field with never a witness to the gospel. Even many Chinese told us about it. That made our hearts ache, so we prayed and prayed and it seems the more we prayed, the more this field was pointed out to us. So we said, "Yes, Lord, we will go and give them the witness." Our funds were barely sufficient to get us here and it has been hard sailing, but we don't mind as long as we feel God is with us.

The lessons we have learned have surely made us stronger in the Lord than we ever were before. It has taken faith beyond measure. We do not count our lives to dear to ourselves if we can please Him. We have done our best since we came here in giving out the gospel message, and we feel that hearts are responding to it. But at the same time we feel that we cannot stay; we must go on. We have sowed the seed, so that now they cannot say that we never came to them or that they had no opportunity to accept. In the spoken word, we have preached as we can, we have given out the written word in tracks and gospels, and we have prayed. What more can we do? The rest we must leave to the Lord.

Many have called us Pioneers, because we came with our family to bring them the gospel. They have never heard of such a thing that foreigners should come with a family to this place that is hated and shunned by everyone. The natives themselves hate this place because of its deadly climate. Many stay here only a few months and then go somewhere else. We are the only American family in town and really the only foreigners. The children are quite an attraction, but they say that we must have lots and lots of money, or we wouldn't have so many children!

We are in the midst of packing again for our next move. We are exercising faith for whatever God sees fit to be our lot. We are looking to Him to supply, as we cannot travel without funds. And eight is quite a number to travel with. We cannot go in the same manner that Brother Standifird did with the native children, as they won't permit foreigners to do what the natives do. We have more responsibilities than most of the missionaries that we have met on the field. They can't understand yet why we should come to China with all these children, but, at least, that has not hindered us from taking the gospel to this needy field. Other people do all the worrying about our children, so I am saved that much; I'll trust the Lord for them!

We understand now more than ever the test of praising the Lord through trials, not knowing what a day may bring forth. I thank Him for not letting us know too far in advance what will happen, but giving us strength each day. So many things face us these days—war, desolation, evacuation, financial extremities, and diver's persecution for the Master's sake. We are pilgrims and strangers in a foreign land. We know what it is to be misunderstood and rejected. We know what it means to be stoned and to find the rocks flying in the open windows of the house. Our lot is not and has not been a flowery bed of ease, as some may think, but we do praise the Lord for the undisturbed peace that He has granted us, and for the love that brings tears of joy into our hearts as we say "yes" to Him and to His will for us and our children. As we look about us and see all this, we pray for grace and for faith, and as we look to Him and catch a glimpse of His face, our faith abounds. We found this little poem that has been a blessing to us and rather expresses our point.

Pressure—Victory

Pressed out of measure, pressed to all lengths,
Pressed so intensely, it seems beyond strength;

Pressed in the body and pressed in the soul,
Pressed in the mine, till dark surges roll

Pressure by foes and pressure by friends
Pressure on pressure, till life nearly ends

Pressed into knowing no helper but God,
Pressed into loving the staff and the rod

Pressed into liberty where nothing clings
Pressed into a faith for impossible things

Pressed into living a life for the Lord,
Pressed into living—a Christ life, outpoured.

Author Unknown

We are glad for the pressure if only God counts us worthy and counts our lives "the Christ life outpoured".

We like the message and the things printed in it. We did enjoy the article entitled Acts 2:4. It is very good. It was very much like that in Alfred's experience. For two years or more he was much filled with the Spirit and the power would rest heavily upon his testimony, but he didn't speak in other tongues. Many told him that we had all God had for him, but he kept right on seeking God, and even after he did receive the liberty of Acts 2:4, he felt he still had to keep on seeking God. The infilling was just a new beginning point in his experience. Today he still feels that he must not stop, but he continues to pray that he may have all God wants him to have.

The Chinese New Year has just ended and the shops are still closed. The celebration was not as elaborate as in a large town, but their worship is very devout. Our prayer is that many may worship the true God as earnestly as these people worship theirs.

Prices have gone up. Sometimes it is a real puzzle to me to figure out just what to buy that will be of nourishment and will be up building, and yet will be within reach of what God sends in. But my trust is in Him. He will give grace at all times for the test. Even our Christmas money could not go for any unnecessary little knickknacks, but just plain food. We have a hard time making people believe we are not made of gold. We must either pay the price they demand, or walk off without buying anything at all, because the shopkeepers don't call a person back as they used to in Yunnanfu. We have not even the simple variety here that we had there. But we do praise the Lord for the privilege of telling them about Jesus, for that is what counts.

The children all send lots of love to you dear ones. They have happy remembrances of many occasions while home. Sometimes they even talk about what they would like to do if the Lord tarries for them to see you all again. We like to see them happy. They have been such good faith kiddies. We thank the Lord for them.

Oh yes! We have made a new discovery. They think we must be rich because we have so many children. The more children, the more money!

We are so glad we can say that we are rich in Christ, as we have partaken of His salvation. We are looking to Him to have His way in our lives.

Yours for the Masters Will and bidding,
The Bernheim Family

• CHAPTER 27 •

April 18, 1938

Dearly beloved in the homeland,

Greetings of love to you all in the precious name of Jesus. God bless you.

"Oh, give thanks unto the Lord; for He is good; because His mercy endureth for ever" (Psalms 118:1).

So much has happened since our last letter that it is difficult to know just what to write. When we left Hokow, the Lord gave us a pleasant reward that filled our hearts with joy, as many of the people to whom we had given the gospel witness came to us, saying they were so sorry to have us leave, and many gave us gifts of native fruit and bread to take with us as we went on our journey. So we know that God did much more than we could possibly see. Surely, in spite of the hardships that we suffered, it paid to take the gospel to them.

When we felt that God was leading us to return to Kunming, we wrote to different ones, asking them where we could stay temporarily. The letters we received were not encouraging. There was no room in the inn, every place was full, it would be impossible (according to them) to rent a place to stay, as even the hotels were crowded and, because of the refugees who were pouring into the city by the thousands. We claimed God's promises, and by faith knew that God had a place for us. We even wept for joy because we knew that God was on our side, even though we did not know where we would be able to stay. And God did the impossible. He gave us a room with ample furniture for camping. The room was large enough so that we could put all of our boxes and baggage inside, too. Hallelujah! It's just like Jesus

Almost everyone was surprised beyond words when we came to town; since they had written, "Don't come, there is no room". God's ways are not man's ways, so we obeyed the Lord. Many were against us, falsely accusing us, but God was on our side, bless His name.

When we met natives to whom we had witnessed before leaving Kunming, they told us how sorry they had been when they had found we had left town, and how glad they were now to see us back. We could tell by their expressions that they really meant it.

The Lord has given us opportunities to give out the gospel in a greater way than before.

Rock is being chiseled to widen the streets in Kunming, and one day a man came to us who had gotten some pieces of rock in his eye while walking along the street, and he wanted Alfred to remove it. The Lord helped Alfred to remove four pieces of this rock with the aid of some cotton, some olive oil and the end of a match. About a week later Alfred made a trip of several days duration into the country. Here he met the same man, who recognized Alfred right away, and immediately told everyone all about him. It was a great witness for the Lord.

Now the people want us to come to this place to live. We feel it is of the Lord, so we are thanking Him for the open door. We knew our stay in Kunming was to be only temporary. Had the Lord not placed us in just the room that he did, perhaps we might not have come in contact with this field. Surely the steps of the righteous are ordered of the Lord.

This field is very dangerous to robber country, and surely in need of the gospel. When Alfred decided to make a trip into that country, a certain Christian man here was very pleased, and told Alfred he would see that he got through safely. So when Alfred reached a certain dangers point, he was surprised to find soldiers and an escort of police awaiting him. They took him all the way, and also escorted him on the return trip. Of course, Alfred would have had no fear, but the natives insisted they wanted our lives protected, so we can bring them the gospel.

We are finding a more friendly feeling among the Chinese people than there was last fall.

The Lord has greatly helped us in learning the Chinese language, so that everyone marvels at the use we have of the language, considering the length of time we have been in China. To God be all the praise and glory.

Our new address will be: Alfred Max Bernheim (missionary), Yanglin, Yunnan Province, SW China.

Yours in love,
The Bernheim Family

(Letters to missionaries should go through our office, as their addresses are often only temporary.)

• CHAPTER 28 •

Yanglin, Yunnan Province, S.W. China

May 9, 1938

Dear Loved Ones,

We are now two days journey northeast of Yunnanfu. The name of the town in which we are located is Ma Kai, but the nearest post office is at Yanglin. I don't know when letters will leave Ma Kai for the post office, but I will write now and send it out at the first opportunity.

The Lord gave us a safe trip. As we told you before, this section is noted for its robbers. Most of the people are afraid to venture outside of town without an escort of soldiers. Nevertheless God escorted our whole family here, and we had no trouble. The horsemen that transported our boxes took special interest in our behalf; they brought the things through safely without our accompanying them, which, we understand, is quite unusual in China. Usually if your belongings get out of your sight, you never know if you will see them again or not. But we have an Almighty God in whom we put all our trust. His Guardian angels were our escort, praise His holy name!

The one that had sent police and soldiers to care for Alfred when he made the trip several weeks ago was out of town. The *Job's comforters* were not a few. They warned us of the brigands that covered the hills. But we felt that God had spoken, and that it was time for us to go.

The horsemen took our boxes, leaving us only a little bedding and a few small things that we would need in case of a stop-over. Some of the men helped us convey the children over the three mountain ranges that we had to cross. They were carried in *whagons*. A *whagon* consists of two long poles with a cross piece that rest on each of the men's shoulders, and a thin rope tied crosswise where one sits. Bedding and extra pieces of baggage are tied in back for a back-rest. The whagons in Yunnanfu look quite comfortable, as they have rainproof roof and sides, but these had no protection whatever. We thanked God for them just the same.

We had to stop in a mud hut when a storm overtook us. We were thankful to reach shelter before we got drenched in the heavy rain that followed. As we were waiting, they pulled a sick man out of the corner and brought him to Alfred. We were reminded of the way they brought the sick to Jesus in Bible days. As we laid hands on the man in the name of the Lord, we felt God's mighty power. Many people had taken refuge from the storm in that little hut, so they were all gathered around us, enjoying the little meeting as we prayed for the one that was sick. Only God knows the end of that storm stop-over.

As we crossed the mountains, we could see what a wonderful place it was for brigands, among the rocks and trees and underbrush. Hallelujah, we had no fear, knowing that our God went before us. Alfred took a different route that he said looked even more dangerous. Some in Yunnanfu said they would never venture out on such territory themselves; say nothing about taking the children. But we couldn't catch the vision of fear.

As we neared Ma Kai, it was getting late, but it was not dark enough to hide the two rainbows God had placed in the sky, reminding us of His covenant with Noah. We took that as a promise for ourselves, and claimed His blessing. The stars appeared at last just as the men had lost the road and started off in the wrong direction. The cuckoo sang it's good night song as, safe and tired, we reached the place of our present abode, so glad that God had been with us. Praise His holy name.

We are finding it rather hard to set up housekeeping. There are so many curious eyes, wondering about the way foreigners do things. However, the worst things are the flies, mosquitoes and fleas that make their yearly round. The natives don't mind them, but I haven't got used to them yet! They are such disease carriers. We covet your prayers.

Alfred is up and around, but still far from strong. Although he seems to have victory over the severe attacks, yet he has spells of weakness from the malaria, occasionally. The children are well and robust looking. Lois has a cold which is probably due to teething. Something has happened to my ears that hinders my hearing. All sounds, even though right by my ears, sound as if they were very far away. I am looking to the great Physician.

Divine healing is new everywhere we go. Many have heard the name of Jesus as the God that the foreigners worship. They come to us asking for medicine, as they want something to aid them in their many diseases. We answer them, "No, we haven't any medicine, because we trust Jesus. Jesus is able to heal. Let us pray". This is a surprise to them. They have heard more about the medicine of the foreigners that about the Great Physician. We covet your prayers most earnestly that God's power will be poured out among the people in a mighty way. It is God they need. He is the only remedy for their sufferings. We know that when Christ comes into their lives all will be different in their souls and bodies.

It has been a miracle and a mystery to us the way the Lord has multiplied the money for our traveling and living expenses this year. All the prices are so much higher than they were, some three times as high. It is impossible to rent a house in Yunnanfu at the present for less than $45.00 American money per month, and it costs $7.00 American money for a single room. The reason for the high rent and other prices is that war refugees who have been pouring into Yunnan province, thinking they would be safe here from the war, only to find that the enemy follows them. Most places are equipped with dugouts in which to hide in case of bombing, which they expect at any time.

The high prices prevail not only in the city but also in the country. Where we are now, we find the food prices even higher than in Yunnanfu in some lines. There is no milk at all. We use the daylight saving plan to save coal oil as it is so high, and we did not have sufficient funds to bring a supply with us. This will help as long as it is summer, and we trust the Lord to supply when the days get shorter. He has never failed us yet. We are not living on the imported goods and luxurious that others feel they must have. And we don't grumble at having the same menu over and over. We eat what the Lord provides with thanksgiving. We feel that we are in His will.

A terrible war raging between the Tibetans and Chinese is causing many missionaries to leave their posts.

We can reach about six villages from Ma Kai. There are many other places that Alfred will be able to contact by going and staying as long as the Lord leads. How he wishes that Brother Jones were here to help him in this work!

On market days crowds of people come to buy and sell. It is then that the children have a great opportunity to witness for the Master. They hold a meeting, singing and quoting scripture to the people, in one place, then go on to a different part of the market, until all of the people have heard the gospel.

It has been raining the last four days, so we are glad that we arrived here and got settled before the rains got started. It would have been very disagreeable, too, in the room in which we were living in Yunnanfu, during such a rainy period. We feel that the Lord has timed our coming and going, hallelujah!

Yours in the Master's Service,
The Bernheim Family

(Here is a special note to insert in the Philadelphian message newspaper regarding the financial support of the missionaries in China)

We realize that our country is passing through a time of financial depression, but is that sufficient reason why missionaries should go hungry? Perhaps everyone could sacrifice just a little bit more than they have in the past, that God's workers might have the bare necessities of life.

The Bernheim's are supported entirely by donations sent by the readers of this paper. They have no other means of support. Let us not fail them at this time.

Because these devoted souls never complain, we are certain that few of our readers realize that privations they are enduring, not only due to conditions in the country where they are, but also due to a lack of financial support from America. It is hard to do one's best work for God on an empty stomach. Let us not impair our servant's usefulness by our failure to supply their needs!

• CHAPTER 29 •

Ma Kai, Yanglin, Yunnan Province SW China

May 27, 1938

Dear Loved Ones in the Homeland,

"Great is the Lord, and greatly to be praised; and His greatness is unsearchable" (Psalms 145:3). Praise the Lord for the unsearchable riches of Christ! Hallelujah! How we praise the Lord because His grace has made us partakers of that riches, even His salvation. To know Him is LIFE. We do enjoy the life that He enables us to live.

We thank Him for the rain, both natural and spiritual. For two weeks we have had rain almost every day. That was needed to enable the country people to plant their rice. But we do thank the Lord for holding the rain back until we have completed our journey to this place. To you in America who can travel rain or shine that may not sound so very important, but if you could see the roads in this land and realize the dangers of traveling in rainy weather, you too would rejoice that God took us safely over those dangerous mountain trails before their real rain set in.

In spite of the rain, we and the children have already gone to several villages with the message of God's love. The crowd gathers even before the singing begins. One day as the children and Alfred were starting out, they were stopped in our own village and asked to sing before going on to the other villages. The people hear the gospel in song as well as in testimony, and know that we are serving the true and living God. We do pray that these messages who will go forth with the power of the Holy Spirit and will bring real conviction upon the people.

Last Sunday, although it was raining hard all day, we had two good meetings indoors. One meeting was just for children. The room was filled with twenty or thirty children, besides several older folks that came to listen also. I told them of Jesus and some of the things He did while here on earth. The next day when the children heard Esther playing the organ just for her own practice, a whole crowd gathered again and wanted to know if it was time to have *lee bi*, or a worship meeting.

This Sunday service for adults was also attended by a good number. Some were tribe's people that came from quite a distance, a different type than I had seen before. Their clothing was sackcloth. Some of their women do their hair in a horn shape, like the shape of an ice cream cone, just above the middle of their forehead. They all listened attentively to the gospel message. These people need prayer. Our hearts cry out, "Send a Holy Ghost revival that this people might know the true God and salvation through Jesus' precious blood!" Will you not join us in this prayer?

These blessings have not been without their trials. Most of the time I have been partially deaf. For a while I seemed to have almost complete victory and was praising God for it, but then became almost deaf again. But I am praising God just the same, for I know that He is able.

Alfred asks you to especially pray for his eyesight. Since he has been ill so much, it is hard for him to read print unless it is very large. Last week his lower set of teeth broke in half, so he has much discomfort in trying to eat food. The devil knows just how to keep Alfred from gaining the strength he should have. For a long time he was too sick to eat, and now that he feels quite well, he isn't able to chew the food, and he feels that it doesn't do him much good without chewing. Yet he is rejoicing in the Lord, pressing on to greater victories for the Master.

Alfred says that it is no wonder that Christ sweat drops of blood in the battle against Satan and in the garden, and if we don't put forth that same zeal and effort in our prayers and our life as we stand on Satan's ground, proclaiming life and liberty to the captives, we will surely go under. We know that God will not permit more than we can bear, so we rejoice in the victory of our Lord and Savior Jesus Christ

The children are doing some real witnessing, and are making good use of their scripture versus and songs. Some of the native children follow them as they go from village to village, and joining in singing the songs. The older people come out from their mud huts to listen. It always amuses us when they lift up one thumb to us and say "It is good". We tell them that it is Jesus that is good.

Until one comes to China and views the land for himself, he can have no real idea of the condition, or what kind of people he may be working among. We have been among some Chinese that are so well to do that they change their wearing apparel three are four times a day. If the missionary is not dressed respectably, they will consider him a beggar and not a teacher of truth. Even the poorest class of people, who expect their teachers to be on a higher level than themselves. So anyone that comes to work amongst these people should bring some good clothing.

I could use many of the Sunday school cards, the small attendance cards, or postcards with birthday greetings and such like to give out to the children in the children's meetings. I am using about twenty-five every Sunday and I am afraid my small supplied won't last very long.

We rejoice in the God of our salvation, for He is greater than all. We are looking unto Him and looking forward.

Your co-workers in the Master's Service,
The Bernheim Family

• CHAPTER 30 •

CHINESE KITCHEN DESCRIBED

June 19, 1938

Dear Loved Ones,

"That wilt show me the path of life; in thy presence is fullness of joy; at Thy right hand there are pleasures forevermore" (Psalms16:11). How do we praise the Lord for His presence with us! He truly gives us joy, yes fullness of joy and pleasures, hallelujah!

When the Lord told us to come to Ma Kai, He gave us Isaiah 30: 21, saying "This is the way, walk ye in it." We obeyed and walked into the open door before us. Our own desires would not have sent us here, but the will of the Master overruled: when we know His will, it is our pleasure to say "Yes, Lord." Although we may not understand the purpose, it is for us to be obedient to the call. We have proved everywhere we have gone that God never fails to go before us. Hallelujah!

To show how God is working, I must first tell you some of our surroundings. The reason I do not tell more of the conditions under which we live is because I do not like to tell too much about the hard part of missionary life. When we willingly gave ourselves to Him who died for us, we said "yes" with our whole heart, and we do not expect to take anything off the altar. We want to make our gift for God as large as possible; ourselves, our life, our all, are His, to use and to send at His own pleasure. As we often say to one another, it is only our reasonable service, for we feel we have given up nothing as yet for the Master's sake; He has done all the giving up.

Would you like to come with me for a visit to the *kitchen*, a Chinese kitchen? First you will see the water trough, surrounded by mud which must be more or less stepped into every time you want some water. On one side is a long table, where stand the dishes used in cooking with the rice steamer and some bowls. In the middle of the room (if we may call in a room) is the Chinese stove. It consists of three large *goes* (the things the cooking is done in), made of iron in the shape of a wash bowl and about as big around as a washtub. One of the *goes* is used for dishwater, another to cook the pig food and the third for their own cooking, frying and steaming.

The first thing that you, as a foreigner will notice, are the *middle clouds*, the flies, so thick that they almost make a cloud. In fact, you cannot see the wall because of them.

In the farthest corner is a small pile of mud which is a Chinese charcoal stove. If I told you that this is where the foreign lady must do her cooking, you would probably turn right about face, because before you reach it, you must first step over the fire pile, a large pile of the ashes that more often than not is smoking and will continue to do so all day. This is where the cook puts the rinds for the pig, and peas or beans or anything else that needs to be cooked all day and then will probably still be too hard for you or me to eat and call it done!

A man is sitting there who will probably stay there most of the time you are cooking. He is scratching himself from head to toe and looking for *live stock* in his clothing, but he stops now and then to come and peer into your kettle to see what you are cooking. If you do not want him to be at your side continually, it would be wise for you to get him a bowl and put in a sample of your food.

But who is this that we see coming? And what is he trying to say? He is, well, we shall call him *Salt*, as that is what we first thought his name was. He is really called Dumb Person. Dear old Salt! He carries the water, washes the dishes, feeds the pig and does anything you ask him to do. He is all smiles, because he knows you are cooking, perhaps making some *emergency bread* or frying a pancake. You cannot resist his longing smile, so you give him some of your food, while he is telling you all about something: it may be the big pigs, it may be the weeds he has dug, it may be the weather, but you will not find out for sure at your first visit; however, his speech is improving so sometimes we may be able to understand him better.

If you should be using your pressure cooker, it will be examined by everyone that comes. Nine out of ten visitors come to the kitchen to light their pipes, and you must warn them that your foreign kettle is very hot. They cannot resist examining the clock on the cooker and before you rid yourself of them, you will probably have told them what you are cooking have explained everything in detail. All this will be pronounced "very good." You may be sure that sooner or later they will return with a friend that they may see the foreigners down in the kitchen.

Becky Croasmun

Should it be a rainy day, as most of our days have been, you will inhale smoke and red pepper all the while you are doing your cooking. The wind blows the rain into your face, and probably the rain will leak right down into your open kettle and the pan in which you are making gravy.

And the mud stove, to our despair, was not very sturdy, and soon we had no stove at all on which to cook. Finally we were presented with an old oil can, which we fixed up with mud and a little iron, so we could continue cooking.

The kitchen adjoins the pig pen, where the horses and mules are also kept. The pigs are allowed to visit the kitchen as often as they please. So is the cat, and she delights in tasting any dishes that are left open.

Among the interesting people that we see regularly are the coffin maker and his wife, the grandmother, and the milk mother, who nurses the baby; also the cook and the horsemen and workmen.

In this kitchen we have witnessed much for the Lord, telling of Jesus power to save and to heal. We have told them many things about ourselves and the differences between China and America. They still continue to marvel over our six children, holding up one thumb and saying, "What a good father!" We have told them that it is Jesus that is good, so, after a conference among themselves, as they marveled over many things, they decided it must be so: it is because the foreign people believe in Jesus that He gives them the peace and joy of having children, both sons and daughters, surrounding them.

In spite of all the criticism we have had from missionary leaders in this country because we attempted to follow God in China with six children, yet it is through the children that we have been able to do most of our witnessing for the Master.

As I said before, God is working, and now it seems that we will be able to have a new kitchen, away from the pigs, and the mud holes, away from the red pepper and the smoke, away from the dirty filth that has accumulated in that place through the years. We did not grumble, but by His grace stood faithfully that which was our lot. The people will still be able to come in for their visits and to hear the Master's story in our new kitchen, but we will have cleaner surroundings in which to do our work. Praise the Lord!

The meetings in the villages continue. The crowds that gathered for regular services are also increasing in number. We are praying that the Holy Spirit will do a real work.

The main Christian lady of this town, who lives in the same house that we do, told me the other day that they had so much greater peace since we came here. They have suffered much criticism from the foreign missionaries who, instead of helping them, have just dragged them down. They feel that we are different from other missionaries that they have known. Please pray that the light of the infilling of the Holy Spirit may be opened to their hearts.

The Lord is giving us many open doors to witness for Him. The tribes' people are asking for a testament in their own language, so we have sent for some.

It would have done your souls good to have been in our last Sunday morning service. Someone asked if they knew the song Jesus Loves Me, This I Know. One man answered in a hearty voice, "Recognized-because Jesus loves me". That was the answer, only spoken in Chinese. Although dressed in rags and sackcloth, he was proud and happy because Jesus loved him. He encouraged all the others to sing heartily and they did. Our little room was crowded and so was the courtyard as the people listened to the songs and the Word of God as it went forth. We feel so helpless even after we have done our best. We know that whatever is done, it will be God and not us that does the work, and yet we, like Jesus, feel that virtue and has gone from us when a meeting is over. Praise the Lord!

Yours in His Loving Service,
The Bernheim family

• CHAPTER 31 •

Yanglin, Yunnan Province
Southwest China

June 30, 1938

Dear Loved Ones,

There are many little points of everyday happenings that I have often thought you dear ones in America might be interested in, but my time is so busy that I do not get many of them in my letters. Yet even the little things show how good and powerful our dear Lord is to hear and answer prayer.

Always the first thing to do when arriving in a new place is to see what can be bought there and at what price. One market day we discovered a lady selling honey. Honey is out of season now, and the price she asked for it was really much more than it was worth, but we felt that we needed something like that to put on the kiddies bread, as they had had nothing on their bread at all. The honey is not sold in cakes but is kept in a jar, and they weigh out the amount you want and put it into your own vessel. We had no kettle with us, and by the time we went home and came back again with our kettle, the woman, honey and all were gone. We looked for her for several market days, but she did not come back. We felt a little sorry because we did not get the honey, but at the same time felt it must be God's plan as the price she was asking was really too much. The Chinese always make it a business to raise the price when a foreigner wants to buy anything, especially if they think you really want the article. Well one day our landlady presented us with a gift of about three pounds of honey. Praise the Lord! Wasn't that just like Jesus? We would not have bought more than one pound at the price that was asked, but God gave us three times as much as we could have bought. And how the children have enjoyed that honey!

I had heard much about the good food served by the Chinese on special occasions, but I had never been invited to such a feast. The food they serve every day is usually very simple, and I was hungry for something different. Again the Lord answered the desire of my heart. One day the landlady asked that we cook no breakfast, but have some of their food, as it was a national holiday and she was fixing some special dishes. Although it was not just what we expected, yet it tasted very good. A few days later, someone who was having a birthday party ask us to eat food. It surely was a real feast and prepared in a very tasty way. Had it not been prepared by Christians, one might have thought that the food had been offered idols, but there are no idols in our compound. Prayer is offered to the Lord before eating food. Praise His name, and there are scripture portions inside and out, so that everybody who can read Chinese characters, know that within these walls are people who worship the true God.

Another way in which people here have shown us great kindness is that when they noticed that we were very careful in spending our money and that our mail was not coming through as it should, they offered to please be allowed to loan us money until we heard from you dear ones in America. This proved to be a great blessing from the Lord as it tided us over until we heard from you and from the bank, and could cash a check again.

It has been a real miracle the way the Lord has seen as through in our finances the last eight months. Although everything was expensive in Hokow, yet when we felt that we were to go back to Kunming, we counted on our money and found we had just money enough to go back on. Another way that the Lord saved us money was that the dear ones who rented us the room in Kunming refuse to accept any money for it. Praise the Lord for His goodness to us.

Now for a little about the family. The children have all grown in the two years since we left America. Mark is a big boy, full of dreams, who loves to cook and to sing. He especially likes to sing to the Chinese in the villages. He doesn't seem to have a care or a burden, or to take anything very seriously, but he is a great help, and does many things to help the missionary work along.

Esther is still her motherly self. She is serious and studious, and her ambitions are all *God ward*. She is, I think, the best of us all in Chinese understanding, and the people always understand her when she speaks.

David is very different from Mark. He is quiet, serious, studious and attentive, good in Chinese like the rest, and loved by everybody. Lately he has been tested in his body, but we know that God is able to deliver. Please pray for him.

Ruth is a very happy good girl, who likes to study quite well and to sing for Jesus in Chinese. She is a real big sister to Lois, and can drive Lois's rare tears away quicker than anyone else in the family. Ruth has not been well lately either, but Jesus is that Physician. Today Ruth pulled a tooth, so she feels quite big.

Missionary Johnnie is as full of life as ever, not very serious, but he loves the Lord in his four year old way. He is still Mother's boy, and always stays close to me when other folks come around. When we came to MaKai, it was dark so we could not see, and things, even to big people, can look very spooky when arriving in the dark, but Johnnie was quick to remark, "Is this where we are going to live"? The first thing I saw when we arrived here was a room full of coffins, which would make most folks shiver in the dark, but we knew they were harmless, and thought perhaps they were empty, although we didn't know.

Lois is quite different from anything Johnnie or Ruth were at her age. She is a very serious, good little baby, and very rarely cries even if she takes a tumble. The natives think she is perfect. She is careful about saying anything around them; she will look at them, but not talk, although she speaks both English and Chinese.

Alfred and I haven't changed much, except, as I told you some time ago, we are both rather thin. But our souls can't get lean when we have such a wonderful Savior. Praise the Lord!

God is doing what men counts impossible. Just recently in this province, the eyes of the blind, the ears of the deaf, and the tongues of the dumb are being opened and loosed to the glory of God. This has happened right among people who have looked down upon us for trusting God for ourselves and our children. Praise the Lord. He knows just how to show his power.

The only meat we can get here is pork and that only once or sometimes twice a week. This is no place for those who can't eat a little pork once in awhile, unless they who are good vegetarians.

And the vegetables are not many. But, as Mark says, "The Lord makes everything taste good". We haven't a food grumbler in the family, and that surely makes it a good deal easier for us, too.

We tried planting a little garden of our own, but it has not been very successful. I expect we will have one mess of peas and the same of beans. Nothing else grew. But praise the Lord; we will be able to buy corn in the fall as there is a large field of it just back of the house.

Another thing that has been a blessing is that we have been able to buy a little wheat here and have it ground for flour in one of the neighboring villages. It makes good flour after you get used to using it, and the Lord has taught me a lot along those lines. I use a hop starter, and the bread taste good, at least to us.

Our house here is supposed to have windows in it, but as yet it has none. The frames are in but not the glass. The birds fly in and out at their own pleasure.

Furniture, such as shelves and drawers, is possible to have and most people have some, but we do not. Our furniture consists almost solely of our horseboxes. I put four of them up in the corner of the bedroom to form some shelves, and Alfred nailed the lids on with stiff cloth in the place of hinges so the lid makes the door to keep the rats and mice out (if they don't gnaw a hole in the boxes). Yesterday a mouse was making a nest in Alfred's shoe while he was wearing his rubber boots on account of the rain. The landlady has loaned us a table and four ancient to chairs.

They are so uncomfortable that I prefer to sit on the horseboxes when I write a letter.

The cuckoo sings before daylight, and often at night when the stars are coming out, it sings its goodnight song. There are mountains surrounding us. We have a nice view from our roof, which is higher than the roofs of most of the houses around us. We can see much of the little valley, and have counted eight villages that we can see from our roof. When I mentioned that to Mrs. Lee, she laughed and said that there are over thirty hidden around the curves and amongst the rolling hills that are quite close, and there are numerous others that cannot be reached by foot but we could go to by horse or carriers. So we have even a larger territory than we thought we had.

A mysterious band of soldiers went through here yesterday and wanted to take possession of our compound. The landlady was successful in getting them to go on. They had many horses loaded with guns and ammunition. We need your prayers. Alfred said they reminded him of the old saying, "loaded for bear". But God is loading us up with more power in Him for whatever may come.

Your letters make our hearts glad beyond words; the salutations of our representatives in China bring tears of love and joy to us and make us forget the trials that have been ours. After all, they are nothing, compared to what our blessed Lord suffered. We are glad for all the hard places that we have been able to cross because we see that these things make us stronger from what is ahead.

I believe we will stay here longer than we did HoKow, as we have a larger field to launch out amongst. The tribes that we reach here are quite different from those we met there. The results of our work may never be fully known to us, but that does not matter, for God will not overlook it. Praise the Lord.

Yours in His Service,
The Bernheim Family

• CHAPTER 32 •

July 23, 1938

Dear Loved Ones in the Homeland,

"The Lord on high is mightier than the noise of many waters, yea, than the mighty waves of the sea" (Psalms 93:4). We are so glad that He is also mightier than the noise of the airships that we hear overhead. Our landlady, who has boys going to school in Kunming, just came in to tell us that in a letter just received from them, they said they have been warned that bombing of the city was to take place soon. Early this morning, although it was so cloudy that we could not see them, we heard airplanes coming from that direction. Airplanes are so rare that the sound of them puts a stir in the hearts of all people, but we that trust the Lord lift up our hearts in prayer to Him, knowing that He is mightier than all.

The latest war news is that old people and anyone who with small children have been advised to leave Kunming (Yunnanfu). We thank God He warned us and caused us to move. Many of the foreigners there laughed at us when we moved as God led us, but now some have already remarked that they were glad we were not in the city at the present time. We praise God that we feel we have made all our moves according to His plan and choosing. We trusted the Lord for our plans in the homeland, and how much more necessary it is to trust Him here!

Alfred recently went on a preaching tour; going farther than it would be possible to take the whole family. As the weather had been very changeable, he went prepared for rain, wearing high boots and a raincoat. He had many opportunities to witness for the Master and met a very friendly spirit among the people. God showed forth His power to care for him all the way.

In the course of his journey he had to cross a river whose banks were overflowed in many places. The stream of water flowed so strongly that it took the horse off its feet and almost carried it downstream. Although the horse went down in the water, Alfred managed to stick on. The Lord had a native just on the spot, who was crossing the river, too, and he helped get the horse and Alfred out of the river. So praise the Lord, there was no harm done except for a few wet clothes.

One night he was invited to stay with a number of officials who were assembled for a council meeting. They insisted that he eat with them at their table, and some of them pulled hair like a bunch of school children arguing who would have the honor of sitting next to him. When they went to bed, the official's all were arguing about where to have him sleep. He went to sleep in one bed, but they decided it was not a good enough place for him to sleep, so they made him move. He finally slept in a nice bed all enclosed with mosquito netting. When he first went to bed, he hid his boots in a blanket at the foot of the bed, as he wanted to be sure and have them in the morning, for he is not used to going barefoot like some of the natives. Remember that we are living in the heart of a bandit country where to find your boots missing would be but a small thing to them. He had to explain to them that he could not eat the hard foods because his teeth were broken. They told him that whatever he wanted; scrambled eggs, noodles or anything that he could eat, would be prepared for him. He enjoyed their hospitality, but left the next morning to carry the gospel to the regions beyond.

He went through one place on the return trip that was heavily guarded where all travelers were searched by police and soldiers. Although they asked for his Chinese name, they did not search his clothing as they did others. They questioned him closely about the trail he was planning to take, as from that point on he would be traveling alone, for there are not many who would dare to travel that way without a guard of police and soldiers. Neither would we without God, but when He is our companion, we have nothing to fear and nothing to lose. Sometime later as he was crossing a high mountain peak, he noticed an airplane circling around and around seemingly following the trail he was taking. The airplane followed him until he was in sight of the valley that led toward home.

Several days were spent it walking, as he did not have a horse all the way. The mountains that he crossed were so steep and the trails so slippery that he felt safer on foot than he would on the back of a frisky horse, where a slip means death. The rain and the storms that we have had almost continually since the first part of May have not made the mountain trail any safer. But, praise God, Alfred arrived home safely, and bubbling over with the joy that the Lord gave him as a reward for his going forth, doing his best to give forth the gospel witness and sow the seeds of eternal life. He was glad to be able to take off the heavy boots and relieve his aching, blistered feet, but he said "When Jesus goes with me, I'll go anywhere".

We do thank you all for the offerings that you have been sending to us. May God bless and reward every giver is our prayer. If we have done anything in China to glorify the Master, you, too, shall have your part of the reward. We may not see all now, but when God rewards the faithful, we shall see what God has done. We do appreciate your prayers. Without prayer we could not stand. We ourselves spend many sleepless nights in prayer pouring out our very life that God may ever have His way. Praise God for the victory that He gives.

Yours in His Vineyard
The Bernheim Family

● CHAPTER 33 ●

Yanglin, Ma Kai, S.W. China

January 1, 1939

Dear Loved Ones in the Homeland.

"Oh sing unto the Lord a new song; sing unto the Lord all the earth" (Psalms 96:1).

We also are singing unto the Lord for all the love that He has bestowed upon us. Bless His dear name.

Although, when this letter reaches you, the New Year will be well on its way, yet it may interest you to know how we spent Christmas. Christmas was different this year than any we have observed before, either in China or America. Other years in China, Mr. Bernheim was confined to bed with sickness, but this year we were glad that he was able to be up and around with us. Just as a family affair, that was the most precious gift that we could have had this year.

As in America children always look forward to Christmas Day, so we find it here. Christmas Day seems to have a special meaning and even the native children began to look forward to it. It's falling on Sunday seemed to add to the interest of the day. We wanted to show the people just what a Christian holiday was and we prayed that God would make the day a blessing and would cause the people to really know the true God. We wanted them to have a glimpse of the Savior that was born to save them.

On Christmas Eve, at Ma Kai, our landlord had a scaffold erected in the market place. A large box with Chinese lanterns around it was hoisted on top of the scaffold. Out of this box came the Christmas story in the form of fireworks. I am sure most of you who did not think of fireworks as something with which to celebrate Christmas, but it was really beautifully displayed. A thousand or more people gathered to see these fireworks. Our young co-worker told the people the gospel story from the Manger to the Cross as the different fireworks were displayed.

Christmas Day was very busy. Many of the people from the outlying districts and other tribes had stayed overnight in order to be with us on Christmas Day. We had morning worship before breakfast in the church room. A really spiritual message was preached and the Christmas songs were sung. Breakfast was served in the courtyard, so no one was compelled to leave for meals. After breakfast we held another meeting. We took the doors out of the church, so that all the people in the courtyard could hear.

For two weeks Mrs. Li and I have been teaching the children Christmas songs and drilling them in acting out the Christmas story. Mrs. Li felt that if the natives can see the Christmas story acted, they would be impressed. It was no small thing to train the children to do just what they should at the proper time and in the proper way. We all had to laugh at the way they would try to do their part. But God help them all so that on Christmas Day each one presented his particular part as nearly perfect as I ever saw anything in China. From the angels' salutation to Mary to Herod's slaying of the children in Bethlehem the story was acted out. Then every child present received a treat of rice balls. The evening meal was also served in the courtyard. Everyone felt that this Christmas was really different from any other.

We decorated the church room with paper flowers, paper chains, and papers representing different national flags. In the front of the room was a large paper heart with the words, "I am the way, the truth and the life" printed on a cross in the center of it, with paper twisted around it to represent the glory. It does look very nice, and it blesses my soul to see the people read the words. How we long to see them all saved. We can but tell them and pray. God alone can save them.

Our young native evangelist is surely on fire for God. He preaches the Word straight from the shoulder. We marvel at the wisdom and understanding God has given him concerning the scriptures, considering the darkness in which he was raised. We thank God that He can raise up such to glorify His name. While he was gone during the month of November, a number of souls that he contacted really repented of their sins. In some places the people are begging for workers to come to them to give them soul food, as they want to repent and go on with God.

The tribe people that attend our services from time to time are very encouraging. They have in their possession twenty Testaments and are calling for more. When the weather permits, the evangelist is going down to them and we are hoping that Brother Bernheim will be able to go, too. He has been feeling quite well lately. However, the weather has been too cold to take any extended trips.

We thank you all for your prayers and offerings that make it possible for us to give these people the gospel. May the dear Lord reward you is our prayer. Oh, our thanks seem so small; they do not half express our feelings of love to you all! But God can do for you that which we cannot and bless you, till your soul will be more and more overflowing with that love and glory that only God can give. May he lead and bless us all this year of 1939, and should He call us home, may we be ready and be found faithful in whatever place He may have put us in His vineyard.

The American Consul advises all citizens, especially women and children to flee to places of safety, during these perilous days. Our trust is in God. We must stand in the gap and point dying souls to the Lamb of God that takes away the sins of the world.

Yours in the Service of the King
The Bernheim Family

• CHAPTER 34 •

Songling, Yunnan Province, S.W. China

May 25, 1939

Dear Loved Ones,

The Lord is my Rock, my refuge, my strength and my all in all. What a blessed privilege to have something solid to stand upon. This is just what Jesus means to us. What would it be if, in times of trouble and despair, we were like those all around us who have no hope and no comfort? Praise God, we have a refuge in the day of trouble.

The last two weeks have not brought anything of special interest, yet we have seen that God is on the throne. People continue to listen to the Gospel with big eyes and long ears (the Chinese expression for listening closely) as we tell them the sweet story of a loving Savior. We pray that the Holy Spirit will do that which we cannot do and reveal God to them in His fullness that they may find peace and forgiveness of sins through His precious blood.

Several times we have known that robbers were prowling around, but God has kept them from entering the house. It is common to meet men carrying daggers, sometimes concealed and sometimes dangling in the open as they want to show how bold they are. Our hearts are filled with praise that God can let us walk among such people unafraid and boldly declare the Gospel of Christ. Nevertheless, we feel the need of your prayers as the darkness is very great. We often say that if it were not for those praying for us, thus holding up our feeble hands and weak knees, we would surely go under. We well know that you also have your trials in the home land, so I say unto you also "…look up… for our redemption draweth nigh" (Luke 21:28)

The enemy has attacked both of us with illness during the last two weeks, but our ever present Physician has delivered us from the power of the enemy, so we are feeling better again, and although our strength is not as it should be, we are praising the Lord for victory. The children are well. Truly it is blessed to serve a Savior who never fails and who never leaves us alone.

Lovingly in His Service,
The Bernheim Family.

● CHAPTER 35 ●

June 3, 1939

Dear Ones,

We just received your letter telling of the home going of our dear Brother Ellis. The sadness it gives us would be unbearable if it were not for the hope of the resurrection and the soon coming of our precious Savior when we, too, shall be with Him. Thank God for that blessed hope.

Truly it can be said of our Brother Ellis that he has fought a good fight, he has finished the course, he has kept the faith, and praise God, he has also received the crown that is laid up for him.

Although it brings sadness, we are not surprised, for we have felt that there was a change in things there. We felt that somebody was no longer praying for us, and we felt also the need of praying for you so much more than usual.

The pressure against us here is so great we hardly know which way to turn. Yet God is so near and precious, and we know He is working. His word shall not return unto Him void, but it shall accomplish that whereunto it was sent.

None of us are sick at present, although we are not as strong physically as we would like to be. Perhaps this is partly due to the sudden changes in the weather. For a few days it was very hot and now it is very cold; it is raining now but I hope it will be a little warmer soon, for the wind seems to have gone down.

Alfred had to be an amateur dentist not long ago. One of my teeth abscessed and pained me day and night for four days until finally I could stand it no longer. Alfred got hold of it with his pliers, which wasn't an easy thing to do, as the top of it had broken off some time ago and he had to get way down in the skin to get hold of it. The root was an inch long down under the gums and there was a long abscess besides; there was almost nothing to get hold of above the gums, and it was wedged in between two other teeth; but our great Physician helped him to pull it, and it came out without any pain whatever. No experienced painless dentist could have had any better success. It is a miracle that it pulled so easily, as even the dentists at home have had a hard time to pull my teeth, breaking them off and having to dig out the pieces afterward. I surely praise the Lord for it. Although we were away from all help naturally, yet God did it, better than any natural help could have done it.

Summer should bring us a change of diet. Potatoes and a little native fruit should be on the market within the next few months. The children found a few wild berries a few days ago, not like anything at home, but they were good for a change. I have tried in vain to get either cow or goat's milk, but the natives use neither. They apparently don't know how to milk never having seen it done. I have even offered to do the milking myself it they would produce an animal, but all to no avail.

I know you will praise the Lord that thus far He has stretched the offerings sent us to meet our needs, or, rather, to get the things purchasable here, and we have learned to get along without the things we cannot get. We can get on the market here: rice; white radishes; sometimes pork, which often is not fit to eat; eggs, once in a while; wheat to grind into flour; a little native brown sugar; salt and pepper; and we bought some soda in Kunming. With these things we manage to set the table day by day. We are thankful for good appetites, and I think I have said before there isn't a food grumbler in the family, but each one enjoys his portion and thanks the Lord for it. A good missionary stomach means a lot. We believe that in every test God is preparing us for things to come. We don't know what the future holds for us, but we can joyfully trust Him, as He doeth all things well.

In the Service of the King,
The Bernheim Family

• CHAPTER 36 •

June 18, 1939

Dear Loved ones:

Thanks be unto God which gives us the victory through our Lord Jesus Christ.

The past two weeks have, in a way, brought us much darkness, as Brother Bernheim took very sick just after I wrote the last letter, and most of the children have also been ill. But our ever-present Physician, who never leaves or forsakes us, has raised us all up again. I don't know what we would do without Jesus, so near and so precious, in these days.

This is now the rainy season, but we take advantage of the brief spells of nice weather to go out to witness for the Lord. Sometimes it seems as if the Lord holds back the rain until we return home. Just before Alfred took sick, he and Mark went to a place about twenty miles from here on a market day where some of the people had never seen a white person before; no matter where they stopped, the people gathered about them, and they took advantage of that fact to tell them about the Lord.

We have told you that robbers are plentiful in this country. One evening one was bold enough to enter our house. She waited her chance and when the native boy left for a few minutes, she entered his room and gathered up his clothes, bedding and a bag of rice. When the boy returned, the thief was hiding in a corner.

Although it was too dark to see her, he heard her kick something as she went out, so he called out and followed her. In the front room she dropped the blankets, by the door she dropped the clothing, and as she ran up the muddy lane the boy caught her, grabbed her head dress and, after a tussle, rescued the bag of rice. The thief fled. The total gain of her loot was worth about $5.00 in Chinese paper money and her head dress which she lost in the battle is valued at $20.00 paper money. We thank the Lord that He helped the boy get back the rice and clothing and blankets. The blankets were ours, and no doubt, she thought all the rest were ours too. The neighbors and landlady soon came to the scene, and in the darkness they gave the woman the worst calling down anyone could have! Of course, she did not hear it, but they had to give vent to their feelings in Chinese fashion, all but our boy who is a Christian and was thanking the Lord that he had his possessions back again.

We continually covet your prayers, as we do not know what will befall us next, but in this we are confident; nothing shall happen without our Father's knowing it, and His grace is sufficient for all things.

Yours in His service,
The Bernheim's

• CHAPTER 37 •

Souls seeking God in Song Ling

Songling, Yunnan Province S.W. China

August 9, 1939

Dear Loved Ones at Home and Abroad,

"Thou preparest a table before me . . . my cup runneth over" (Psalms 23:5). Praise the Lord. Our cup is so full that it seems as if we cannot praise Him enough. I know our dear prayer warriors will rejoice with us.

First, God has wonderfully answered prayer in sending us native co-workers, two young men with lives consecrated to God, willing to give all for the poor, lost souls of their countrymen. One perhaps will not stay in this vicinity very long, but the other believes God wants him to labor in this section for a time, at least.

Their aim is to teach the Gospel to every creature so plainly and simply that it will almost force them to see the right from wrong and force them to decide whom they will serve, the true and living God or Satan with all his false gods. We believe it is just such men as these who are needed in this place and we thank God for sending them to us.

Secondly, we praise God because the people seem to have come to a place of decision. They can see that the worship of idols is just a trick of the devil to lead them to hell. A goodly number have knelt before the Lord, saying that they wanted to believe on Him for forgiveness of sins. Some have confessed their sins, some have ceased burning incense, and others are not afraid to witness to their false teachers. Some join us in daily prayers and many come for teaching every night. Do you wonder that our cups are running over with the joy of the Lord?

Thirdly, we want to ask you to keep on praying, for you all know that when God begins to work, the devil works also. We trust in Him who is stronger than Satan, in Him who has said, "All power is given unto me in heaven and earth: lo, I am with you always, even unto the end of the world" (Matthew 28:18). We can see the enemy working on every hand. One of the devil's teachers came to see us, intending to start a fight, but the Lord's power so locked his mouth that he was able to speak hardly a word. God, through one of his servants poured forth the Gospel in greater power and force than I have seen before in China. Praise the dear Lord!

Last Sunday I prayed for five or more people who were afflicted in various ways, one demon possessed. They all left with smiles on their faces, begging me not to forget them, and thanking me in ceremonious bows. I ask that you dear ones will remember them in your prayers, too.

Last week Alfred went to one of the adjacent towns intending to cash a check, but found he could not do so. Since we were almost completely out of funds, it was necessary for him to go to Kunming. The Lord was with him, although the truck in which he was riding broke down and he was compelled to stay overnight in a very undesirable village where he had a wonderful chance to witness for the Lord. He wanted to return home as soon as possible, but there were no buses traveling, as gasoline is not being shipped in here because of the war.

On Saturday and Sunday, although we here at home did not know that Alfred was in Kunming, the Lord told us to pray especially for the city. We also prayed for a bright clear Sunday so that people from other villages would not be hindered from coming to services. The day here was perfectly clear, which is rare for this season of the year. Alfred told us later that the day in Kunming started out very bright and clear. At dinner time the warning whistle began to blow and the people began to scream in horror as they ran wildly in every direction, for the enemy planes were just overhead. At the same moment, storm clouds gathered and a deluge of rain fell from heaven. For about three and a half hours, the battle raged, but God protected His own.

Alfred's soul was in perfect peace, and for some time he stood outside the gate warning the people to trust in God and exhorting the Christians to lay aside all fear and rest in the Lord, telling them not to be afraid, for we at home were praying for them. (Yes, thank God, we were praying for Kunming and he had the assurance from God that we were praying, too.) We do thank God for the rain that He sent so that there was little damage to the city. The Chinese put up a valiant defense. So far, every time the enemy has come, intending to destroy Kunming, God has in a mighty way come to the rescue and won the battle for the city. When Alfred returned, it was quite a testimony to the people here, for many of them knew that we were praying for Kunming just at the time of the bombing.

Becky Croasmun

As you all know, this is robber territory. Are any of the robbers ever caught? Yes and the sentence is death. Just a few weeks ago, a robber who had been very vicious was caught and in order to keep him from making an escape, his legs were broken until the day of execution. We did not know about the execution, but felt led to go to a certain village to preach on a certain day. We were told that the robber was to be killed in the same manner as others, cut in pieces alive. I shuddered as I heard of it. I, for one, did not want to see it, nor did I want my children to witness such a scene. When we reached the village, we began to sing and soon a large crowd gathered around us. Suddenly the soldier's whistle began to blow. We wondered if our audience would all flee and run to the scene. A few turned to follow the soldiers, but many were more interested in what we were saying, and while we were pausing to catch our breath between sentences, someone called out, "Preach some more! Don't stop!" So preach we did. A few left, but more came to listen, till about three different groups had heard the Gospel that day. Our throats were tired from talking so long, but seed was sown or the Master.

Market day is always chosen for the day of execution, so as to show the people the result of sin.

When the two native workers came to us, God marvelously protected them from the hands of robbers. They saw the victims of two violent robberies committed that day. The robbers had cut their legs and the ligaments in the joints so seriously that those men will never be able to walk again. Do you wonder that we plead for your prayers, as we witness for the Master here? There can hardly be a darker spot in the world.

• CHAPTER 38 •

August 21, 1939

The devil has been hard after us. Last week I was ill. I am better now, but still feel a trifle weak. David is not well now and our tribe's boy has been sick for several days.

God is still working. Yesterday four knelt for salvation, and several the other weeks. Perhaps there has been twenty or more altogether. I would not go so far as to say that they are saved, but they have taken a step toward expressing their desire to serve God. Some are bound by opium, but we know God's grace is sufficient.

We have prayed for God's protection over us here, and we heard a bit of interesting news the other day, as some people here were questioning us about what kind of weapons we carry to protect ourselves. Several people claim they have heard gun shots coming from our bedroom window and have seen the bullets fly. One reported having heard at least three shots, while another heard as high as ten. They say it happened at noonday, just at the lunch hour. We wonder what the meaning of it is. We know that our God still lives and answers prayer. Our Captain is King of Kings and Lord of Lords, even in the heart of a robber country.

We want to express our humble thanks to you all in the name of the Lord for so faithfully sending offerings to us as we witness for God here. May He reward you all. Please accept these few lines as a personal thank letter from us, as no one knows how occupied we are daily in our Master's business here. You will rejoice to know, that, in spite of the extreme increase in prices, God is taking care of us and all our helpers. We have nothing whereof to complain, but much whereof to rejoice. We thank you all for your prayers.

Yours in His Vineyard,
The Bernheim Family
Emily Bernheim

• CHAPTER 39 •

September 13, 1939

Dear Loved Ones,

Greetings to you all in Jesus' precious name. We are so glad to be able to report victory and we know you are rejoicing with us that at last we can see a little of the work that God has wrought. We feel well repaid for having obeyed the voice of the Lord to carry the Gospel to a land of darkness. It is one thing to travel through a land of robbers, but it is quite another thing to go and live in their midst, daily proclaiming the Gospel. We thank God that He has enabled us to live in a robber country and to witness to His name.

It is great joy to see men and women coming to the Lord in this land of darkness. Oh such darkness! Darkness! Darkness that words fail to describe! Can you imagine a people so bound by superstition that no one can get married in a rented house; that a woman cannot give birth to a child inside a house, but must go out in the yard and stay in a straw hut for three or four days; and if someone dies, the relatives cannot sleep on beds or sit on stools—the floor is the only place permitted them. There are so many kinds of darkness and superstition that Satan has these people bound with.

We do praise God that a goodly number are coming to the Lord. Some are already beginning to tell others what God has done for them and are bringing others of their family to believe on the

Lord also. From two to five kneel at every service, and on Sunday our little room is packed with listeners.

One old lady who lives about fifteen Chinese miles from here surely has a *hot heart* for God. One Saturday she came to us, bringing her two daughters and two old women. The daughters had been to see us before, but the two old women had never before seen a white person. She brought them especially so they should believe on the Lord. They did; and we had to find some way to keep them over night for the Sunday service. We had no beds to offer them and had only bedding enough for our own use, but as the natives are not in the habit of sleeping too comfortably, they said they would be happy if they could only sleep on the floor. The landlady, who has also surrendered to the Lord, came to the rescue by giving them straw carpets to sleep on and under. We offered to give them food. So after two meetings on Saturday, with supper between, six dear women slept on the floor to await the Sunday services. And praise the Lord! It was a blessed day wherein several more knelt before the Lord.

We earnestly plead with you to pray as never before for these believers, for the devil is hot on their trail bringing many afflictions upon them. We keep busy praying for first one and then another. I don't understand half their ailments, but we have a Savior who understands and heals, bless His dear name.

The people are calling for the Gospel in many places, so one worker is going out with Alfred and Mark and our tribal boy tomorrow, Lord willing. The other evangelist is in another part for a few days, while I hold the fort at home with the smaller children.

We thank all of you, who have so faithfully given to our support that the Gospel may be given forth in this dark land, and we know when the Lord of the Harvest rewards the faithful, you too, shall have your part for both prayers and offerings.

Yours in His Vineyard,
The Bernheim Family

• CHAPTER 40 •

Bernheim's moving to a New Location

October 2, 1939

Dear Ones,

Greetings in our dear Savior's name.

Our new address will be Hsi Men Kai, Chan 1, Yunnan Province, S.W. China. We are launching out to spread the Gospel there and will leave the work here in charge of one of the native evangelists. We have been in this place for over six months, and we do praise God for the blessed fruit that He has given in the last few months. But since this is such a large field with no one else to carry the Gospel, we feel that it is time for us to enlarge our borders so that others may hear the Gospel, too. This new station will be more centrally located than where we are now so that we will be able to reach more people without making the long journeys that separate the family for days at a time and that also mean a greater expense and unpleasant places to stay during the trip. Of course, it will be necessary to make some trips, but this new place has many advantages in location.

When our two co-workers came to us this summer, one expected to stay only for a short time, but God has revealed to him to stay and preach the Gospel to these needy people. We truly thank God that the work will go on here just the same under his direction.

We feel the time is short and we want to reach as many as possible before the coming of the Lord.

Securing this new place is really a miracle, as almost every place that can be bought or rented is taken by refugees.

We know what it means to go to a new place where we must plow up the ground for the Master; where we will have to fight against and break down all sorts of evil powers; superstition against the foreigners, darkness untold; where we will have to set up housekeeping all over again, which is not so easy in China. Thank God, we do not have to go in our own strength, for we could never do it. But He is our life and our strength, our salvation, and when he goes before us, we can easily follow His footsteps.

Can you imagine how your floor would look if it had never been cleaned in eighteen or twenty years? The house we are living in now is about that old, and the floors had never been cleaned until we moved in last spring. Perhaps you remember my telling you about our having to scrape the dirt off the walls and ceiling with a scraper or shovel. That is the task that is facing us again as we move into this new place.

As the Lord supplies, we will have to put up a new house, as the dwelling place at present is not very good and is much too small. This place will be a home for us and for the missionaries the Lord sends.

In all, we can say that God is working every day and in every way; and so is the devil. We earnestly covet your prayers, both for the place to which we are going, and for the work we are leaving behind. Some of the circumstances that face these young Christians are heart-breaking, but we know God is on the throne.

Love to all in Jesus' dear name,
The Bernheim Family

Letter from Esther Bernheim
Age 12

Dear Philadelphian Sunday school,

P'ing an—Peace be unto you.

I am writing the story of my trip with Daddy. We got packed up and started about six o'clock in the morning, for the trip before us was 120 li, or Chinese miles. It rained, so that the road was not easy to walk in. You never saw such mud as we have here in China! Suck dirty, sticky mud that you just slip all over.

One block from our home is a graveyard. The coffins here are not like those in America, but are just heavy boards about four inches thick, pasted together. Sometimes they dig a shallow hole in burying the coffins and sometimes not; the hole is never very deep and often one can see the coffin sticking out of the ground. Most of the time dirt is piled on top of the coffin, so that the graveyard is all little hills. I slipped and fell in the mud in the graveyard. We went through three graveyards on our trip. Some people won't go near the graveyards for fear of the dead, but we are not afraid when Jesus is with us. A dead person can do no harm; it is the living ones that one has to watch!

We walked in the mud and rain all day. Our shoes got all muddy and our legs too. The water in our shoes made a squeaky noise when we walked. Just before we got to our stopping place, we took a bath in a rice field to wash some of the mud off our legs and clothes; only we took the bath with our clothes on.

When we reached Chan I, we were tired, hungry, cold and blistered. We soon changed into some clean, dry clothes and would have felt comfortable, but for our blistered feet. It rained 7 days and nights and that made lots of mud. I never had a wetter trip than this in all my history!

On the second of September the Chinese celebrate the moons birthday. They worship the moon and burn paper to it. They call the paper money, but you couldn't buy a drop of water with that money, much less anything else!

We bought some eggs the other day with some real money, but all though the eggs were two for a dollar. Two of the eggs were bad. They had the money and we had the rotten eggs. Do you think they would give us our money back? No, never.

The inn in which we stayed had an idol worship table upstairs in the room in which we slept. When they worshipped the moon, they also offered incense to the idols. My cot was right in front of the idol table, so when the people came to worship, they asked me to please move my cot so they could worship. We moved it in the middle of the room, and as the room was very small, daddy put his cot up on top of the board bed. That was funny, as it made a five story outfit, counting the mosquito net! We sang songs about Jesus on one side of the cot, while they offered food and worshipped the idols on the other side. When they got through, our evangelist preached to them.

We stayed in that town and witnessed for the Lord several days, and got our new home located. We hope we will be able to get it cleaned up. It is too dirty for words as it stands!

On our way home, the Lord was with us in a wonderful way. Daddy and I were walking alone along a certain trail, as our helpers had taken a different road that they thought perhaps would be a shortcut, when all of a sudden we heard an awful tramping and rustling of bushes behind us. There was a group of men who stopped when we looked around, but soon came running again and caught up with us. They crowded in, surrounding us, so that soon there would be no place for us to turn. Daddy knew it was time to say something, as they were all vicious men, armed with knives and ropes, so he stepped to the side of the trail, and I did too, then daddy lifted his arm and said "Now you run!" (Hsein Tsai Ni Pow.) Well, praise God, the Lord made those people run, and we were safe. Our helpers had seen it from the other trail and were almost scared to death. They said that the devil surely possessed those men to do us harm, but God delivered us. Just a few days ago, a man was cut to pieces by a robber just a little ways from our house, just a short time after we had been along that very same road.

The roads were a little dryer coming home. I was surely glad to see Momma again. Lois was so glad to see me home again that she crawled all over me. I was glad to see her, too, for she is such a dear little sister. I'm still nursing blisters.

Please pray for us as we shine for Jesus.

Lovingly,
Esther Bernheim

• CHAPTER 41 •

Chan I. Yunnan Province. S.W. China

June 04, 1940

Greetings to all the Saints,

"Not unto us, O Lord, not unto us, but unto Thy name give glory for Thy mercy and for Thy truths sake. Wherefore, should the heathen say, "where is now their God?" But our God is in the heavens: He hath done whatsoever He hath pleased" (Psalms 115:1-3).

If you dear ones will just read the whole 115th Psalms, you will note the contrast between those who trust in the true and living God and those who trust in idols. We are so glad that our God can speak for Himself and manifest His power in answer to prayer.

Shortly after our last letter was written, the Lord sent us some more precious souls for His kingdom. It was getting very late one evening, but having been busy all day, we had not yet had our supper (God's work comes first, ourselves last), when, in the midst of preparing food, we heard a knock at the gate. The natives do not like to open gates after nightfall, and some thought, "Who dares to knock at this hour?" But answer we must.

Since there are no windows in gates, we could not see who was standing outside. We called, "Na I ko (who is it?)"

The one outside answered, "It is I." Well, "I" could be anyone, and always in such cases we are expected to recognize them by their voices.

So we apologized, "We do not recognize your voice. Please tell us what you want."

The answer came back, "I believe, and I am sick. I want to pray."

We hurriedly opened the gate, while the natives stood back in wonder, and let the sick man into a side room where he told us his story. Seven years ago in the neighboring province, he had heard the Gospel. He had wanted to believe on Jesus then, but his heart was cold. Education, war and work had kept him away from his home.

Now in distress, sick in body, afraid to die, afraid of hell and not fit for heaven, he had asked the people, "Is there a Gospel hall any place?"

"Oh, yes," someone answered, "such and such a place is the white pastor but what do you want him for?"

"I must go to them. Do not stop me. Come and lead me. I am sick. I cannot find the way alone."

"Oh, it is too late. Wait until tomorrow."

"No, I must go now. I may die and I need prayer. I must go now."

God, he believed, had given him the strength to walk to our place, and he was taking that as a sign that there was a true and living God. If he got well, he felt he must serve Him. He already prayed to be forgiven, but as we prayed for him, he also poured out his heart to God; with fervent amen's to our prayers for him. He said an eternal "yes" to God.

Sunday he came to church, and with him four others who needs must hear the Gospel, the power of God unto salvation.

We give God the glory for revealing Himself unto the heathen.

This last week we managed to enlarge our chapel room, so we hope to be able to accommodate the people better that they won't have to stand in the street.

It is still a little dark, but we will soon add some windows to let in more light.

Continue to pray for us that we may, in that day, hear His "well done."

Yours in His Service,
The Bernheim Family.

• CHAPTER 42 •

June 26, 1940

Dearly Beloved,

The last time I wrote, I believe I told of having to enlarge our chapel. Last Sunday night the chapel was again full and many were outside. A large number came early for special instructions in the Word before the regular service started so before we opened the chapel door, we had the room half full. We thought that perhaps many who came early would not stay throughout the service, but we found that many who came first were the last to leave.

Before we came up this direction, a sister in America dreamed that we were going to a district where we could reach soldiers. This dream is now fulfilled, for we reach many soldiers in this place.

Two soldiers, especially, have come to the services quite regularly. They had heard the Gospel in a hit and miss fashion in the past, and had both adopted Bible names. They had been in the army about ten years and had stayed together, both having come from the same place in the beginning. One day one of them came to us saying that his pal was very ill, dying, he thought, as he could take no food and was spitting blood. The doctor had given him medicine, but he was no better.

Soldiers often die; it is just a matter of one less to feed and clothe. It is nothing to see them gaily carry the dead partner to the graveyard. But these two were special pals, and it would be this man's duty to break the sad news to the relative in a distant province if his friend should die. Was it possible that we could do anything for his pal; did we have some special medicine that keeps us well?

We asked him how long his friend had been ill, as we had noticed he had been missing from services for several Sundays. He told us about two weeks. We asked him if they had prayed at all. No, they had never thought about praying themselves. So we chided him, and also lovingly prayed, both for him and for his sick comrade, then we told him to go back to camp and pray for his pal and to take a firm stand for Christ daily in prayer and testimony.

Last Sunday night both soldiers were at the service, the sick one with a shining face, a heart full of joy, and a testimony, Jesus has raised me from a bed of death. Surely his face was a joy to behold! Christ is the same yesterday and today and forever.

We most humbly send our thanks to you both for the prayers and the offerings that the saints so lovingly have given God's work here. If you would not do your part, we would be weakened in fulfilling our part. Let us all, therefore, continue to be faithful.

Yours in His Service,
The Bernheim Family

From Johnny Bernheim to Our Associate Editor

Sister Bernheim writes Johnny has a letter that Orise wrote him three years ago. He keeps it stored away like it was a gold mine, and has become conscious of the fact that perhaps he had better answer it. So I am to write the letter and he will put his name below.

Johnny is six years old now. His letter follows.

Dear Orise,

I still have your letter that you wrote me three years ago. I like it very much and I keep it with my best things. I am trying to learn how to write hard. I can read one story in the "Sled" book. I wish you were her to be my teacher. Momma is going to give me a Neigh Be [Note: That is a piece of money that comes in five and ten cent pieces and he thinks they are worth millions.—Mrs. Bernheim] for learning to write my name to sign on this letter.

I have a new pencil that Momma says you gave us when we left America. I don't think I remember you or America, but I remember a long, long time ago I was on a great big ship that they tell us came from the United States to China where we now are.

I got a new blue suit. It is made just like the one that came in the box from American. Also my new shoes. I like them very much. They fit me nice, but I only wear them for Sunday or if special company comes. Thank you very much for them.

I am six years old. I sleep with the rest of the children in the same bed, because there aren't enough beds to go around. I am Momma's little miller and sometimes grind flour so she can make biscuits. I got a green baby stool and a pretty little basket. I pray for you when I say my prayers.

We had potato pancakes for lunch, the first time this year. I was servant to carry the pancakes from the stove to the dining room, so they could eat them hot. I ate after everybody else had some first. Then when momma and I ate, Esther baked and Mark was servant. I help wash dishes sometimes.

Goodbye. God Bless you.

Lovingly, Your little Friend
JOHN ALBERT BERNHEIM

• CHAPTER 43 •

Chan I, Yunnan Province, S.W. China

October 2, 1940

Dear Brother and Sister Steelberg:

Greetings in the precious name of Jesus, praise His worthy name again and again. I suppose you often think we have long forgotten you, but praise the Lord we have not, and as long as we see your picture calendar before us we also remember you in our prayers. We feel that we owe you an apology for not have written you a word of thanks for sending us the calendars, but we surely have appreciated them more than tongue can tell. Up until its arrival this year, we would just turn an old calendar to what month happened to be most fitted for the month desired, adding or subtracting the days at the month end as the case may prove to be. Thus we managed until we received your welcomed one. So God bless you a hundred fold is our prayer.

We have been in China over four years at this time. We have had much to learn, and still have. The Lord has been with us in every way, for which we thank and praise His precious name. We have had much to contend with in the line of malaria and sickness, but the Lord has proven Himself all sufficient and healed us all many times. Just a few weeks ago Brother Bernheim was healed of dysentery in the most miraculous way. He had been suffering for about a week getting weaker each day, when one morning while in prayer, He seemed very far away, when he found himself eating and smelling the most delicious butter one could wish for. Then suddenly as it were, returning to earth, he wondered where that delicious butter came from. We can't get either milk or butter in this place. Then he realized he had been feasting at the Lords table. Needless to say, he was healed from that hour and has been gaining strength every day. Oh we have such a wonderful Savior, words fail in thanking and praising Him sufficiently.

Just about a month ago, we had the privilege to bury 18 in water baptism. The Lord surely blessed in the four day convention that we had at that time. These dear ones all returned to their homes in various places round about with the shine of God's love and glory upon their faces. We ask you to all please pray for these Christians. Some are up in years, the oldest being about 75 years old. It means much to leave the old god's of wood and mud, and serve the true and living God, yet as they left, they all sounded the note of victory.

Following this glorious victory, the enemy was stirred. Many Christians were persecuted but thus far have overcome the enemy. As for ourselves, we know not what a day may bring forth. We need much pray, in these days when war is on every hand, everybody is packing for evacuation, not knowing where to go, east or west. No one knows which is the safest way to go. We are just waiting on the Lord to have His way with us. Thus far He has proved himself more than faithful, and we are confident that at this trying time He will never leave us nor forsake us. Much more could be said on this subject, but it is not advisable to write much. But we know God will answer prayer today as in the days of old. Bless His dear name.

We trust these few lines find you in the midst of God's richest blessings. Please excuse the many mistakes. We have had so many disturbances since trying to write this, but God is on the throne. Bless His dear name. How are you all? We pray God bless you every one and give many souls for your hire. Do you receive the Philadelphian Message, who prints our letters to keep in touch with the work of God here? If not, just drop a line to E. G. Watson, North 2019 Division Street, Spokane, Washington, and Sister Watson will be glad to send them to you as they are printed. Will close with much love and prayers for you. Also coveting prayers from you in behalf of the Lords work here.

Yours in His Love and Service,

The Bernheim Family
Alfred Max Bernheim

• CHAPTER 44 •

Chanyl, Yunnan Province, S.W. China

October 12, 1940

Dearly Beloved:

"Unto the upright there ariseth light in the darkness: He is gracious and full of compassion and righteous . . . surely He shall not be moved . . . . He shall not be afraid of evil tidings; His heart is fixed, trusting the Lord." These verses, from Psalms 112, express conditions as we have been facing them these last few weeks. Much of the darkness that surrounds us cannot be written, but God has proved Himself faithful, so that we do not fear evil tidings.

Recently I had to take a trip to Kunming. Conditions in the capital are not very encouraging from a natural point of view, but those who have put their trust in God know that He will protect His own. The children and husband prayed earnestly that there would be no air raids while I was in Kunming, and the Lord answered prayer, as I returned safely without have heard an alarm, although one sounded shortly after I left the city. Scenes of war are not pleasant, and I will not try to describe what has taken place in Kunming. It is wonderful to me that thus far whenever we were called to enter war-torn fields, God has caused all things to be peaceful until we left.

You will wonder are you safe where you are. My answer is that no one is safe if not under the blood. War planes fly over our heads daily. Air raid alarms send the people to the hills, fear falling upon all of them. Our trust is in God, not knowing what a day may bring forth, but knowing that our Father holds all things in His hand and will not permit anything to befall His children that will not work for their good and in some way glorify the Master in the end.

I think I wrote several months ago about the native worker at the Songling district. His mother engaged him to a girl who had never heard the Gospel. Much prayer went up about the matter, and God has wonderfully undertaken. It is much against the custom of the country people to speak to their future wife or husband, all plans being made for the wedding without the young people having a chance to say a word. One day, however, the young man was called to the home of his future mother-in-law. She had heard very little Gospel, but what she had heard had touched her heart, so now she wanted to burn all the idols and dedicate her household to the Lord. Before we heard this, we sent word that the future bride should at least have the opportunity to hear the Gospel and become a Christian, as it is not good Christian custom to marry an unbeliever. The mother, having burned the family idols, was more than willing that her daughter should come and hear the Gospel. So she came. Poor soul, she had never left her mother's doorway before. She had never seen a horse, to say nothing of a truck or an airplane. She didn't even know what a fish was; it just happened that we were able to get some one day. She had never been to market. The first thing she wanted to do was to take a walk to the bus road; she held her breath when we told her that she couldn't go alone because the truck might bump into her and knock her dead. As we told her about the Lord and showed her how the devil had her bound, her heart began to open up. Yes, she would follow Jesus. The first step was to unbind her feet. My own heart ached for the poor girl. We made pair of larger shoes. As the blood tried to circulate, she was hardly able to walk, but God gave the victory, and she is glad to be counted among those that love the Lord.

Dear ones, pray, Pray, PRAY for us all, as you have never prayed before. Pray for all those who have taken a step for the Lord. Join us in doing all you can, for the night cometh when no man can work.

Yours in His Love and Service

The Bernheim Family
Excerpts from a Personal Letter

You perhaps hear more of the real situation of things than we do. We are so glad that we have the assurance of your prayers.

Alfred had a dream not long ago of the grain being in the barn; although he had hoped to help others reap their grain with a large sickle. We cannot say what the definite meaning of this dream may be, but we feel confident that the Lord will have his way.

The railroad has been destroyed. All foreigners are leaving the mission stations. If evacuation becomes necessary, there will be a three months' journey by horse to the edge of Burma, if horses can be secured; if they cannot, we will have to walk. Of course, we are not making any predictions, but just looking to God day by day. The children have their pack sacks all ready, so that if war comes heavy over our heads, we will be ready to go to the hills. All roads are broken and cut off in this section of the country. We can't get through toward the east or the south; war abounds on the north also and the west. But thank God, there is no trouble between God and His children.

I hope to hear from you soon whether or not you received my letter in which I mention the possibility of our coming home in about two years. Now I wonder if perhaps we will meet at home in the air to ever be with the Lord even before that time. The upward look is bright; nothing can hide His shining face.

• CHAPTER 45 •

The Last Letter to the Philadelphia Church office
Written three days before their death

November 2, 1940

On Tuesday, October 29, the Japanese planes suddenly attacked Chanyi. The shooting lasted for at least an hour. The roar of the planes as they passed directly over our heads was terrible. Thank God for His blood that protected us. More raids are expected continually.

The American Consul at this time advises all Americans to return to America as soon as possible. We look to God to have His perfect way with us. I wonder if you received my letter written in August where I wrote that I felt the Lord would have us return home. I naturally thought it would be sometime before June, 1942, when our passport would need to be renewed, but now it looks as if it will be sooner than that.

Someone once said to me, "Why don't you write the folks at home more about the hardships of missionary life?" That is very hard for me to do. Jesus, in His day, said, "The cup that my Father hath given me, shall I not drink it?" So as Jesus drank the bitterness of Gethsemane, we find perfect peace in following Him in what we feel is His calling for us. The road has not been sprinkled with thornless roses. But the Lord has not left us hitherto, and we know He will not forsake us at this time. Perhaps everything is all ready for us, and we have just not heard the final word of it as yet. God's ways are marvelous and past finding out.

I have mentioned in other letters about our health being run down. The Lord has given us supernatural strength during these last few weeks for the new trials that are facing us. I know it is only God's power that is upholding us all. Esther said to me the other day, "Mama, your eyes are all black and sunk in. I can't see your eye-lids!" I knew I had lost some weight, as my thimble is very loose on my finger, much more so than it was before, but I had no idea that my face showed any signs of strain. The Lord has been so near to us that is has been natural to cast the load onto His shoulders. We have felt that He is carrying the load for us in a very precious way.

We long for His perfect will to be done in our lives. Our lives are upon the altar, and also the lives of these precious children that the Lord has given us. We are not afraid of death should it approach us. Yet it seems only advisable that we spare the children the horrors of death and war, if possible. If God opens the way of life to them, and they live for His glory, how much good can be wrought (should the Lord tarry), only He Himself knows. We know God always has need of those who will be faithful. This is our hope for our children as well as ourselves. We pray that should theirs be the future work, God will speedily undertake that none be prematurely cut off.

All meetings must be held at night under war conditions, as should a large crowd be gathered together in the daytime, they would not be able to take refuge in case of an air alarm. Pray for our meetings that, in these testing times, God will reveal to the people their need of a real Savior.

One of the young Christians whose home is many miles away, came last night to see if we were all safe, He gave a good testimony how God had protected his and his uncle's cattle while many of their neighbors' cattle were dying in a plague. These two are trusting God. Please continue to hold them up in prayer. Pray that the Blood will be upon the Christians and all that is theirs, as a witness to the power of the true and living God.

Our faith is stronger than it was when we first came. God has helped us to grow in Him.

Lovingly,
Emily Bernheim

• CHAPTER 46 •

Chan I, Yunnan Province, S W. China

November 4, 1940

Dear ones in the Lord,

"O give thanks unto the Lord; call upon His name; make know His deeds among the people" (Psalms 105:1).

Greetings in our precious Saviors name. How we long to be able to give perfect thanks unto Him and make His deed known among the people.

For over 4 years now we have been standing as a witness to the Gospel, here in the dark land of China. God has been very gracious unto us. We have seen His power manifested in many ways. We have been raised as it were from death ourselves many times. We have seen Gods power poured out in healing touches upon the heathen, we have seen some of them saved, and see them growing daily in the grace and knowledge of the Lord Jesus Christ. The Lord has taken us thru many trials and many victories. The Lord has proved himself faithful. Could we make all His deeds known, it would fill a book. We can but praise such a wonderful Savior, Redeemer and Guide. A Counselor that is closer than a brother.

At this time we wish to express thanks unto you and the any in your assembly that have so faithfully stood by us in prayer and many other ways during all this time. Surely you also shall share in the reward at the harvest, having done what the Lord gave you to do. Had you failed in praying and doing your part, we also would not have had the strength to stand thru the darkness that we at times went thru during these days. As the Lord's coming draweth nigh, we find the battle getting harder. Each day brings us new trials as well as victories. Many of these things cannot be told in a brief letter, but you, who are praying for us, often receive from the Lord the knowledge of our needs and God has never failed us up to this time.

We are at this time however asking you and all the saints to please remember us in special prayer that God may have his perfect way with us at this time. The word has been sent forth that all American citizens especially women and children should return home on account of the serious war conditions that now exist thru this nation. Very few of you know that we are at this time in the direct war zone of this province. It is only the mercies of God that we are alive today. We trust in Him to keep us safe as long as He sees that we have work and witnessing to do. It seems very needful however that within accordance to the advice of American Consular authorities that God speedily undertake and we be able to leave this war province at this time. Thus we ask you to please pray, especially for us and this need. We believe God is able. May the golden vials soon be full of odors, which are the prayers of the saints.

I am sure you are all aware of our home address in Spokane, Washington. Mrs. E.G. Watson, who takes care of our correspondence in the U.S., will be glad to send us any word that you may have. And as it is impossible for us to write personal letter from this far away place without a great expense, she will also be able to keep you informed as to our safety, etc.

May God bless and reward you all is our prayer. Our words fail us in thanking God who has always stood by us, and we are confident that he is just the same today as he has been in the days past. The days of miracles are at hand. Let us look up, be strong in the Lord and do exploits.

Yours in His Love and Service,
Brother and Sister Bernheim and family of 6 children, all in China at this present time.

• CHAPTER 47 •

SPOKANE MISSION IN CHINA RAIDED (AP)

Mrs. Emily Bernheim, 36 and Son, 11, Murdered by Bandits

Spokane members of the Philadelphian Church Association yesterday were waiting anxiously for official confirmation of an Associated Press report that bandits invaded their mission in southwest China, killed two members of the missionary family, and wounded two others.

The report said that the American consulate of Kunming, in Yunnan province, was advised that the dead were Mrs. Emily Bernheim, 36, and her son, David, 11. Seriously wounded was the Rev. Alfred Max Bernheim, husband of the dead woman, and less critically injured was another child. Four other children escaped.

Left for China in 1936

All are from Spokane and left here for China in 1936 to establish the only mission of the church society in the orient. Mrs. Bernheim was born in Spokane and attended Grant school. She was a daughter of Mr. & Mrs. Charles Hasenkrug, who came here from Canada in 1900 and lived at E 1108 Eleventh.

Details of the tragedy were lacking yesterday. Mrs. C.R. Hollandsworth, a sister in Spokane, said she has no information other than that contained in the Associated Press dispatch. Mrs.

Hollandsworth lives in the old Hasenkrug home on Eleventh. Another sister, Mrs. Clifford L. Wells, lives in Dartford, as does a brother, Ed Howell.

The Rev. Mr. Bernheim was a painter in Spokane before he was ordained a minister. Mrs. Bernheim was also ordained by the Philadelphia Church association, which has its headquarters at N 2019 Division in Spokane.

On Burma Road

Chan I, where the Bernheim's established their mission four years ago is about 75 miles from Kunming, which is on the Burma Road from French Indo-China to China proper.

Letters from Mrs. Bernheim to headquarters of the church association indicated she was enthusiastic about her missionary work, despite the hazards which marked the family's daily life.

"Ever since she was a young girl, Emily dreamed of a day when she would go to China as a missionary," her sister, Mrs. Hollandsworth, said yesterday. "It was not, however, until she was the mother of five children that she was able to go. Two days after the family arrived in China a sixth child was born."

A letter written August 2 by Mrs. Bernheim underscored the raids by bandits and lootings which were becoming more and more frequent in the neighborhood of the mission.

Poverty is Appalling

Others spoke of the poverty among the natives. "It is a common thing to see unburied caskets standing around," Mrs. Bernheim wrote. "They have a special field where caskets may be set, for when there are no sons in the family, the corpse is not buried. They don't consider them worth a funeral, especially girls. Do you see the darkness in this land and the need for prayers?"

In her last letter, Mrs. Bernheim announced that the family's passport had been renewed and that it expected to continue work in the Yunnan province field.

SLAIN PARENTS' CHILDREN AIDED (AP)

5 Orphans of Bandit Victims to Come to Spokane

Five youngsters, who were orphaned about two months ago when bandits murdered their parents and a brother during a raid on their mission home in China, will arrive next week in Spokane, where four of them were born.

Their slain parents were the Rev. and Mrs. Alfred Max Bernheim, former Spokane residents, and missionaries for the Philadelphia Church Association. Upon their arrival in Spokane next Friday or Saturday they will be greeted by Mr. and Mrs. C.R. Hollandsworth, E 1108 Eleventh, an uncle and aunt; Mr. and Mrs. Clifford Wells, Dartford, another uncle and aunt, and Ed Howell, Dartford, a third uncle.

The children arrived in San Francisco yesterday aboard the *S.S. President Coolidge* and were taken to Tacoma for a week by an aunt, Mrs. H.W Howell.

Relatives Will Adopt Them

Mrs. Eleta Watson, N 2019 Division of the Philadelphia Church Association, said yesterday the orphans will not lack for a home, their relatives in Spokane and Tacoma having decided to adopt and rear them.

The Bernheim's left Spokane for their Chinese mission post four years ago. Their youngest child was born a few days after their arrival in the orient. Mrs. Bernheim was a daughter to Mr. and Mrs. Charles Hasenkrug who came to Spokane from Canada in 1900.

Passage of the five children, the oldest 14 and the youngest 4, to the United States was made possible by a loan from the American government.

An account of their arrival in Hong Kong and details of the tragedy in which their parents and brother died follows from the December 16, 1940 issue of the South China Morning Post:

The arrival in this colony on December 2, by D.N.A.C plane was Kunming, of the five Bernheim children, recalls of the tragic incident which occurred of Chan-I, about 30 miles north of Kunming on the night of November 5, resulting in the brutal murder of their parents Mr. and Mrs. A.M. Bernheim, and younger brother, David, 11 years old. The five remaining children Mark, 14; Esther, 13; Ruth, 9; John, 7; and Lois, 4, are now staying at the Phillips house on Moody road in Kowloon, awaiting their departure to America on the *President Coolidge*, sailing on December 7.

An interview with the oldest boy, Mark, brought out the essential facts of the incident. The Bernheim's arrived in Yunnan some four years ago, during which time they labored as missionaries in the Kunming area. A little over a year ago they moved to Chan-I, where greater opportunities presented themselves. Here they built a two story house of dirt construction, as well as quarters for their lay evangelist.

Notorious for Bandits

The area has been notorious for bandits, but the missionaries had never been molested and the Bernheim's paid very little attention to the rumors. It was not until a few days before the tragedy that they began to realize that trouble was brewing, in Mark's words, "We began to feel there was a snake in the grass."

Only a few days before there had been great excitement when the C.N.A.C. plane piloted by the late Mr. Kent was compelled to make a forced landing at the Chan-I airport after being pursued by Japanese aircraft, and this was witnessed by Esther. To add to the confusion there were air raids and a threatened Japanese invasion. Most of the people in the community, including the Bernheim's, took refuge in the wooded hills nearby, but returned to their home when the all clear signal was given.

Brutal Attack Described

Shortly before midnight on November 5 the family was aroused from sleep by someone yelling and rapid steps coming up the stairway leading upstairs. By this time Mr. Bernheim was standing at the bedroom door inquiring what was wanted and the reply was, "Money". Without further words Mr. Bernheim was shot in the side and mortally wounded; he died early the following day. Mrs. Bernheim and David met instant death. The other children had marvelous escapes. Mark had taken refuge under the bed. John was still in bed and was struck by a stray bullet in the foot. Otherwise no injury befell the other members.

When asked for a possible motive for the attack, Mark related how that a few days previous one of their Chinese friends had brought them a load of walnuts. Also the same day some packages of Bibles were received by mail, and the rumor circulated that the packages contained currency and this might have encouraged the attack.

Since their arrival in the colony, the American consul general, Addison Southard, has taken a keen interest in the children and has facilitated their expatriation to the United States. Many friends have contributed toward fitting them out for the homeward journey. Dr. and Mrs. C. S. Schoop of the Kwangtung synod office of the Church of Christ in China have been godparents to the children since the night of their arrival.

• CHAPTER 48 •

Our Trip to America
By Esther Bernheim (age 13)

After the robbery, we all went to Kutsing where Miss Julia Clark took care of us for about three weeks. Kutsing is about ten miles from Chanyi. We all enjoyed being with Miss Clark, but we were all glad to leave on December 1st. I am glad we were all packed up the night before, as we got up early the morning of December 1st. The bus was to leave at eight o'clock, but an air raid came and the bus could not move for fear something might happen. It was ten o'clock when we left Kutsing.

We arrived at Kunming at five o'clock. The American Consul met us at the bus stop. A man near the Consul said he would give us a room and beds for the night and the Consul let us eat supper with him because it was late.

The next day there was another air raid and we had to go to the hills again. But the Lord took care of us. It gave us a chance to preach to many people.

That night we all went to the airport and waited for about fifteen minutes for the plane to come in. At five o'clock in the evening we started to fly. Lois was asleep on the plane. Praise the Lord, we were not air sick. The ride was very nice.

We arrived at Hong Kong at eleven o'clock that night. We spent three weeks in Hong Kong. Then we repacked and got ready to leave for America. They said the boat would leave on the twenty-fifth of December, but it actually sailed the twenty-eighth.

We stopped four times in coming to America, first in Shanghai, then two stops in Japan at Kobe and Yokohama, then at Honolulu. Finally we arrived at San Francisco. There were many times on the boat that we might have had an accident but the Lord took care of us and the boat. Praise His name.

We are going to the Grant school now, and we like it very much. All of us are staying with our Aunt and Uncle, Mr. and Mrs. C.R. Hollandsworth. We all hope you will write to us.

Our address is: Mark N. Bernheim, E. 1108 Eleventh Ave. Spokane, Washington

We ask you all to remember us in prayer every day and the people that have given their hearts to the Lord in China. Pray that they may not fall back into their worldly ways. And pray that the people that have not given up the way of the world will.

• CHAPTER 49 •

It Must Have Been His Will
By Orise Watson, The Philadelphian Message

"It must have been God's will or He would not have let it happen," wrote thirteen year-old Esther Bernheim from China, shortly after the robbery that took the lives of her parents and brother. "It must have been His will or He would not have let it happen," she repeated to us a few days ago.

The Bernheim's had been working for almost a year on the construction of a home and mission station where other missionaries could come for training. They had moved into the new house, with its chapel and living quarters for the native evangelist as well as living quarters for themselves, just a few months before the fateful night of November 5th.

Just a day or two before, they had received a shipment of Bibles through the mail and word spread around that the packages contained currency. In the afternoon of November 5th, a Chinese Christian from a neighboring village came to visit them with a friend, bringing a heavy load of walnuts as a gift for the beloved pastor and his family. The children tell us that money is often carried in that way, camouflaged as nuts or some other commodity. Once again the word spread around that the missionaries had received more money.

After all had gone to bed, the Bernheim's were awakened at 11:00 pm by the sound of rapid footsteps coming up the stairs. Mr.

Bernheim stepped to the door of the bedroom and quietly asked the intruders (number about fifteen) what they wanted. "Money", was the reply. Without giving him time to answer them, the robbers shot him in the side, mortally wounding him.

The robbers then shot Mrs. Bernheim, who was still in bed, through the heart, killing her instantly. They turned their guns upon the children who had rushed out when they heard the noise. Eleven year-old David was found later beside his mother's bed, shot through the head at close range. Johnny, who was still in bed, was struck by a stray bullet, wounding his foot. Baby Lois, sleeping next to her mother, was unharmed, although covered with blood. In bathing her the next morning, Esther found where a bullet had just creased the top of her head. The other children had equally marvelous escapes.

We are reminded of the letter that Sister Bernheim wrote just three days before this happened, and her prayer for her children: "Our lives are upon the altar and also the lives of these precious children that the Lord has given us. If God opens the way of life to them and they live for His glory, how much good can be wrought (should the Lord tarry), only He Himself knows. We pray that, should theirs be the future work, God will speedily undertake that none be prematurely cut off."

The bandits, who had stationed guards at every exit of the house to prevent anyone's escaping, grabbed up as much as each one could carry, systematically plundering the house, before leaving. Yet even then, God's hand permitted them to go so far and no farther. Although the Bernheim's did not have the amount of money the robbers thought they had, yet they did have in the house at that time a considerable amount of Chinese currency. The box that contained the money, which was kept in Brother Bernheim's room, was grabbed by the robbers along with many other things, but the next morning the children found the box and money on the floor in another room. In their hasty exit, the robbers had dropped the most important part of their loot. The typewriter too was dropped by the robbers.

For seven long hours, Mark and Esther (fourteen and thirteen years old, respectively) cared for the wounded, comforted the little ones and waited for daybreak. When morning came, they notified the Chinese magistrate. Esther says, "Chinese magistrates never are nice to you except when something like that happens, then they are."

Mr. Bernheim, Johnny and the other children were taken to a mission hospital at Kutsing, ten miles from Chanyi. There Mr. Bernheim underwent an operation from which he seemed to be recovering. However, his body was in such weakened condition from frequent attacks of malaria, he had lost so much blood in the hours before he reached medical care, and the shock of Emily's and David's deaths was so great, that his heart grew steadily weaker and he passed away at 7:00 o'clock the evening of November 7th. Mark said, in telling us about it, "The way the people of the world look at it, he would have lived if we could have taken him to the hospital right away before he had lost so much blood. But we know it must not have been God's will for him to live or God would have healed him anyway'.

Esther's diary for November 7th records, "We had a service at the cemetery for Momma and David today. Daddy just now passed away to heaven. I am sewing." November 8 records the burial service for her Daddy and November 10th, Sunday, another memorial service.

"God is our refuge and strength, a very present help in trouble; therefore will not we fear though the earth be removed and though the mountains be carried into the midst of the sea" (Psalms 46:1, 2). Although the world that these children had known was uprooted and they were suddenly torn from all that they held dear, God still was their "refuge and strength, a very present help in trouble."

At home in Chanyi, whenever both Brother and Sister Bernheim were ill, Mark and Esther managed the household, did the cooking and buying, conducted the preaching services and Bible classes, and did whatever was to be done. Now, with mother and father called up higher, Mark and Esther carried on with what was needed, with a strong faith in the power of God to keep them and to provide for their needs. They closed up the house at Chanyi and disposed of their remaining possessions, Esther finished some needed sewing for the children, and they packed and prepared to leave China, trusting God to make a way.

Mrs. Bernheim had written that it would require a three month trip by horse or on foot if horses could not be secured along the Burma Road for them to get out of China. But God undertook for the children. They were sent from the interior by airplane to Hong Kong, traveling at night because they were crossing over Japanese territory.

In Hong Kong there were outfitted for their trip to America through the donations of clothing and money given them by

Chinese and foreigners of that metropolitan city. The children remember many happy moments of their three weeks' stay in Hong Kong, picnics, sight-seeing trips, and the happy Christmas day planned for them there. Mrs. Shoop, of the Phillips House where they stayed in Hong Kong, writes, "It was such a privilege to have the children in my care for several weeks. They are such wholesome children, are so reasonable and so amenable to reason that it was a real pleasure to do things for them and with them. There must be something very fine in their background. They reveal real strength of character and even of conviction. They made many, many friends here. Esther is a very devoted sister and a good manager. We were constantly being surprised by her knowledge of practical matters. Perhaps the children will tell you that Mark gained thirteen pounds in weight, Esther, twelve pounds; Ruth, ten; John, seven and one-half, and Lois eight pounds during their three weeks here."

On board the boat, the S.S. President Coolidge, a kindergarten class was formed and Esther enjoyed her part in teaching the children. She explained, "Most of the second class passengers were missionaries returning to America. Many of the children were fatherless, but we were the only ones who had lost both mother and father in China."

While the children were still on board the boat en route to San Francisco, the Lord showed four year old Lois, who was born in China and had never seen any of her relatives in this country, that her Aunt Lydia was going to be her Momma. The child is intensely timid and even in China, whenever strangers were around; she clung to Momma and Daddy *like sticky fly paper* as her Mother expressed it. After their death, Lois would allow no one but Esther and Mark to do anything for her. But when she knew that the Aunt Lydia, whom she had never seen, was to be her new Mamma, her little heart was filled with such love that, on the morning of January 27th, when the children stepped from the train in Spokane, after spending a week with their uncle and aunt in Tacoma, and Lois caught a glimpse of her Aunt Lydia, she ran right to her and from that moment refused to be separated from her. The tiny, clinging arms could not be pried loose from their strangle hold around Mrs. Hollandsworth's neck even to have her picture taken. Mrs. Hollandsworth, although several years older, looks quite a bit like her sister, Emily Bernheim. Lois says, "My other Mamma went to heaven. I knew in my little heart that I was coming to a new Mamma."

The children have been kept busy, since their arrival in Spokane, in renewing old friendships and meeting many new friends. To make up for the rather bleak Christmases of interior China, their year has brought many Christmases with gifts and dinners. In spite of all the candy, nuts and good that have been showered upon them since their return, when asked what they would most like to eat if they could have their choice, the unanimous answer was rice. We pray that, as attentions continue to be showered upon them as they witness for the Master, their hearts will be unmoved by the plaudits of the crowd and they will continue as unassumingly as they were in China.

We pray, too, that they may remain unmoved by those who would imply that their God must have taken a vacation from watching over them on the night of November 5th. May they always know as they know today, that "It must have been God's will or He would not have let it happen."

• CHAPTER 50 •

NOT IN VAIN

The following are updates about what has happened in the years following the growing up of the 5 remaining Bernheim children. You may notice there is a change in the spelling of the last name. The author of the information is at the bottom of each letter.

Esther, the eldest of the Bernham daughters, married Delbert Rice in 1950, just before he entered the seminary. They pastored four different congregations of the Evangelical United Brethren Church in Oregon before going to the Philippines as Missionaries in 1956 with their two eldest sons, Harold and Alfred.

After language study they lived in the province of Isabela, the northeastern portion of Luzon, for about 9 years. In that area they provided in-service training for the pastors of the United Church of Christ in the Philippines (UCCP). While there, Esther delivered two more sons, Eugene and Timothy. The two older boys began their formal education in the Philippine public school where the language was mostly Llocano, the language in the churches and in their home.

In 1965 they were called to direct the mission work of the UCCP among the Ikalahan people who lived in the Caraballo and Southern Cordillera Mountains of Northern Luzon.

For this assignment they had to learn the Ikalahan language. Delbert was the first to begin writing the language. It was a tremendous challenge as they guided a holistic evangelistic and development program with the people in spite of the fact that they had almost no funds with which to work.

By 1974 the Ikalahan, with Delbert's help, were able to wrest control of a large section of their ancestral land from the government. The Ikalahan protected that portion of their lands so well that the government developed a Social Forestry Program patterned after the contract that they had signed with the Ikalahan and President Ramos even made it a key program under his administration.

Over the years the Ikalahan, with the help of Esther and Delbert, developed many programs for community benefit while the two congregations that existed when they went to Kalahan in 1965 became more than 40, all pastored by local leaders and self-supporting. One of the programs in Imugan, the village where they live is a Food Processing Factory which uses forest fruit to make high quality jams and jellies. Esther developed the first basic recipes and Delbert turned the recipes into factory recipes and supervised the program for several years. Local leaders are continuing the work.

They also pastored the congregation in Imugan for several years but it has been in the hands of local pastors now for many years.

Their programs attracted national and international attention and they soon became hosts to many groups who wanted to learn from what they had done. Delegations began coming from other parts of the Philippines and from Viet Nam, Cambodia, China, Africa, Indonesia, Malaysia, India and many other countries.

In 1971 they were invited to visit the aboriginal churches on Taiwan. Their daughter, Tynee, at that time, was only a year old and accompanied them. Within a few days Esther began to remember the Mandarin language which she had spoken as a child but had not spoken for half a century. She could often tell Delbert what was going on even though no one had translated for them. In most instances he had to preach through two interpreters because there was never a single person who could speak one of Delbert's languages and the language of the congregation. In spite of that he was able to share with them enough of the theology of evil spirits so that the churches could begin to deal with the problems they had been having with demons.

About 1991 a group of about 20 Chinese came from Yunnan Province and stayed in Imugan for about 5 days to study Agro-forestry. Esther and Delbert were excited, of course, but they were afraid to discuss directly their interest in Yunnan with the delegation members because at least one party functionary was in the group but they had no way of knowing which one. To discuss the life of a Christian missionary in such a situation might endanger any Christians in the group. By that time, of course, Esther had forgotten how to speak Mandarin. Most members of the delegation seemed to be less than 40 years old, so they could not have known the Bernham's anyway.

On the third day of their visit, however, Delbert was watching the Ikalahan boys play basketball and a member of the Chinese delegation, a man who seemed to be about 55 years old, came and stood beside him. Neither one said anything for a few minutes although they smiled at each other. Finally the man tapped Delbert on the elbow to attract his attention. With signs and an English vocabulary of less than 20 words he asked Delbert if he was a Christian. When Delbert excitedly replied "Me Christian." The old man responded, with equal excitement, "Me also Christian."

That conversation could not continue for lack of an interpreter but Delbert was finally able to contact a Canadian who knew the situation on Yunnan. "Yes," he informed Delbert. "Most people in this part of Yunnan are Christians. The communist party tried to stamp it out but they could not. The house churches continued to multiply and grow and they still continue".

That was not a very long conversation and neither Delbert nor Esther has been able to go to Yunnan, but it is plain to see that the martyrdom of three Bernham's was not in vain. The church is there and it continues to grow because the Holy Spirit is continuing His work there.

Esther and Delbert finally retired, that is what they called it, in 1996 but they continue to live in Imugan where they have lived since 1965. Esther has been overcome with Alzheimer's disease and can no longer participate in the work but Delbert continues to be active in helping the more than 50 congregations that have been established. He also works throughout the Philippines and South Asia helping upland communities. He is an advisor to many government officials and official in several thriving non government organizations which help tribal peoples such as the Ikalahan as they confront modern society. Stimulated by Esther's support for more than 50 years and the example set by her parents and his, he continues to help these tribal societies confront modern problems by using their ancient skills and culture.

In addition to his visits to the communities and churches he also write books, several of which have been published in English, Llocano and Ikalahan. God continues to use them as he used their parents.

Esther went home to be with the Lord in February, 2008. (Written by Delbert Rice, Esther's husband).

****

All my life I knew that the greatest purpose in life was being a strong Christian. Whether in school or on the job, I wanted my life to count for Jesus Christ in the best possible way.

Our parents instilled in us the importance and necessity of trusting the Lord Jesus in all situations daily. This was evident as we needed God's guidance as pioneer missionaries in remote parts of China, where there was neither electricity, well water or any clean water, (nor white people). We'd pray for daily protection and guidance. The areas were so dangerous, filled with robbers, bandits and murderers. It was so natural to pray and fully trust God for every situation.

I believe the experience in China taught us to fully rely on God for direction in our lives.

The night of the murders we all knew immediately that we should try to get back to Spokane, Washington to be raised by our mother's sister Lydia and her husband, Reverend Charles Hollandsworth. Our parents told us many times in the previous years that if anything happened to both of them; try to get back to America to live with our Aunt Lydia and Uncle Charlie. They would raise us as Christians and that we should try and stay all together.

The Hollandsworth's were devout Christians and raised us all in the Christian faith as our parents had.

We can never thank them enough for allowing us all to live with them and their two boys. Really I guess we five stole the two upper bedrooms from our cousins, James and Luke. We were all one big happy family and we thank them all for the love and care and fun times we shared. I call James and Luke "Brother Cousins" and I think they like it!

I wouldn't trade the "China experience" for anything. It has taught me how to be a committed Christian as well as to appreciate things more. I'm sure I couldn't have had a better teacher.

As for my life after high school, my years were spent as a working girl, always having a good church to attend faithfully. I liked being a helper in all kinds of departments of the church, whether teaching kids or painting walls or window trim or whatever.

Finally at age 42 I married a find Christian man from San Jose, California. We lived in San Jose until 1989, retired and moved to Salem, Oregon.

I love singing and playing the harmonica at church on the worship team for Jesus. I still remember and can sing lots of Chinese songs. I told myself I should write out with English sounds and sing them on tape lest they be lost from our family altogether.

I feel extremely blessed having been raised in a missionary family and by Aunt Lydia and Uncle Charlie. And a "Huge THANK YOU JESUS!"

(Written by Ruthie Bernham Smiley)

****

What impresses me most about my parents was they sold everything they owned and went to China. While there they walked back into the interior hundreds of miles with us kids. That dedication is so rare. I remember walking at night and seeing the fires of the bandits. My mother led me to the Lord when I was 4 years old. I have lived for the Lord ever since.

Aunt Lydia and Uncle Charlie along with their two boys, James and Luke took us in. Uncle Charlie had no job and lived on faith. He walked to town everyday and ministered to whomever the Lord sent his way. Some businessmen might hand him some money and more than likely he handed someone money who was in greater need. To take on five more kids to feed, we learned to live by miracles. I remember once when we came home there were ten 100 pound sacks of potatoes on the porch.

After graduation from High School I attended Cascade College and earned a degree in English and Education. I taught at the Eugene Bible College, and then taught high school for four years, junior high for two years and then I went into counseling. I counseled in the junior high for two years and then worked as a counselor at Lane Community College for twelve years and then became the director of counseling for twelve years and also taught counseling part time at the University of Oregon.

I was married to Dionne for twenty three and half years before she died from cancer in 1975. We had two daughters, Lynn and Lori. Lynn is married to Randy and has two children a girl and a boy. Lori is married to Dave and they have two boys.

In 1976 I married Peggy. We were married for eighteen years until her death from cancer. We had a daughter Jennifer. In 1998 I married Jan and we have been happily married for ten years. She has two children a boy and a girl.

I have run 13 marathons including the Boston Marathon.

I have been close to death many times but the Lord always delivered me. Once my appendix burst and once in college I lost control of my car. There were at least ten times I have faced death. It has only been by the divine protection of the Lord that has brought me through.

(Written by John Bernham)

****

Growing up in the home of Aunt Lydia and Uncle Charlie was a great blessing. Can you imagine having five extra children move into your home after having only two? We were welcomed with open arms! James and Luke (their sons) are like my brothers. Never once did they make me feel like I wasn't part of their family.

I am so thankful for my heritage of faith in God. Aunt Lydia and Uncle Charlie were great people of faith. They taught us that God would supply all of our needs! If we needed healing, or maybe a new tricycle, we just prayed and believed God for it! God did supply all of our needs!

I married a wonderful man, Joe Coats, and we celebrated our fiftieth anniversary this year! We have had an awesome life together. He was a career military man so we moved many times. Every time we moved we would find a church home and become active in that church. Joe and I have two sons, Philip and Joel. Phil is a successful attorney. He has two sons. Joel is retired from the Navy. He has two sons. (Written by Lois Bernham Coats)

****

My Earliest Memory is:

There are five Children coming to the states from China. They came by boat, on the President Coolidge, to San Francisco, California. It was decided that my mother's brother, Henry would go to San Francisco and meet them and bring them to Spokane, WA by train. They came to Spokane, where the government was going to decide where to place them. Nobody wanted all five. Henry wanted John & Ruth, but Lydia, my mother, would take Lois.

I had one brother named Luke; he is 5 years younger than I. I was 17 when they came from China. I worked the night shift during my last year of school at Broadview Dairy, making Ice Cream to help support the family.

My Father, Charles R. Hollandsworth, was a faith preacher. He fasted and prayed several days then said to my brother and me, "I feel we will get all five!" When the judge in the Federal Building had a hearing they were arguing, where to go with them, my Father spoke up and said he will take all five. The judge wanted to know the kind of job he had. Dad answered he was a faith preacher. They could come and check on them when they wanted. He knew they would be taken care of. We had a six room house with one bathroom.

My brother and I shared one room, Mark and John shared the attic, Esther and Ruth shared the other room and Lois was in the bedroom with my folks. In the summer time we boys all slept outside until November.

We went fishing often out at Newman Lake, where the Watson's had a place on the Lake. Watson's had been the correspondents for Bernham's while they were in China. We had many happy times growing up. I was going to Lewis & Clark High School at the time. One night I came by Boges Bakery to pick some bread, when the manager called me over to see if our family had the children from China, I said "Yes", so he told me "you stop every Friday night on your way home from school and bring 35 cents and ask for chicken bread". For over a year, I stopped by, and asked for the chicken bread. It was a 100 lb flour sack filled with bread, cakes, and rolls. It was Christmas every Friday night, all the children waited for me to come with the treats

Written by James Hollandsworth, age 82 the oldest son of Charles & Lydia Hollandsworth.

****

Mark (my father), the oldest son, join the army and then married Betty Ruth. They had four children, Philip, Rebecca, David, and Stephen. Mark was a licensed minister in the Church of God and pastored churches in Oregon, and in Washington. He was also bi-vocational working in road construction, the lumber industry and at the end of his life he worked as a welder. By this time his health began to deteriorate and in 1976 he went home to be with the Lord. His wife Betty Ruth became a pastor after his death and pastored a Church of God in Bellingham, Washington and later in Everett, Washington for 13 years before her death in 1996.

Philip was married and has two daughters Karma and Krickett and a son Jason. He was a school teacher for twenty years. He passed away from cancer in May of 2008. He lived in Connecticut with his wife Carol. David lives in Washington and has a son Mark and is retired from the shipyards. Stephen lives in Panama and is retired military. He has three children Raisa, Stephen and Tiffany. I (author of this book), am a licensed minister with the Church of God and have pastored in Texas and have ministered throughout the country. I am a widow and have one daughter, Bridgett who has six children and a son, Randal who has three children. My husband was a minister until his death in 2003.

Ministry is in my blood. From the time I was 15, I felt a call of God on my life. Since that time I have done all I felt God was asking me to do.

My earliest memory, going to church, learning God's Word and then teaching others has been the focus of my life. My mom preached nightly in a downtown mission in Spokane, Washington when I was very young. My father, Mark, played his accordion and sang. My father was given his accordion by an evangelist not long after he returned from China (see photo). That accordion was a major part of our lives. He played it during every service. He played it holding street meetings. He played it and sang and preached at nursing homes. Everything about my life growing up always revolved around some sort of ministry.

Ministry was not forgotten. After my father's death, my mother, Betty Ruth, continued in ministry and she pastored churches in Bellingham and Everett, Washington.

My husband, R.G., and I under the discipleship of my mother went into the ministry. During that time, we were associate pastors under her. We then went to Seattle and pastored the same church my father had been the pastor of in the 70's. We had a very large congregation of Romani Gypsies. For ten years we ministered as missionaries to these people. During that time we went on two missionary trips to Nicaragua helping to build a medical clinic.

When my husband died in 2003, I felt like my ministry was also over. However God had different plans. I have pastored a church in Texas for a year and then God moved me on. I am in transition and wondering what God has for me. Even in my senior years, I feel the call of God even greater than I did at 15. I know I will minister till I step into the portals of Heaven.

This ministry legacy goes on. My daughter also is pursuing ministry and my granddaughter is getting ready to go to Bible

College and nursing school to become a medical missionary. This legacy is not taken lightly. It is an important part of my heritage. Why God chose me is only known to him. I remember being so shy that I would literally be sick at the thought of standing up in front of people. The first time at age 4, I was supposed to sing, standing in front of everyone for a moment, and then running to mom in tears. When I went to pastor a church by myself, I remember on the first Sunday, walking across the front of the church before anyone came and saying to God, "What have I gotten myself into?" God called me and no matter how inadequate I may feel I will do what he asked because I know that there is a great legacy that must continue. And so my Legacy of Faith continues through four generations.

(Written by Rebecca (Becky) Croasmun, Mark's daughter)

• ABOUT THE AUTHOR •

Teacher, Minister, Musician, Mother, Grandmother, and Mentor, Becky Croasmun has been in some venue of ministry for 45 years. She has taught children, teens and adults. She has spoken at women's retreats, worked in youth camps, spoken on the mission field and pastored alongside her husband of 29 years before he went home to be with the Lord.

She has endured the pain of losing a loved one through death, the tragedy of having a child turn to drugs and has personally had the experience of a doctor telling her she has an incurable life threatening disease. Through all of this, she has discovered how to have faith and hope that even when bad things happen, life's dreams are shattered, God is still in control we must hang on to the last THREAD OF HOPE, God is there, He loves you and He will not fail.

Becky is currently residing in South Texas and is planning seminars and retreats to minister to those hurting along with her daughter, Bridgett. She speaks regularly for churches and women's groups.

To schedule Becky to speak for your church or special group contact her at:

brcroasmun@yahoo.com